NETWORK ENGINEER'S BIBLE

MASTERING 100 PROTOCOLS FOR COMMUNICATION, MANAGEMENT, AND SECURITY

4 BOOKS IN 1

BOOK 1
FOUNDATIONS OF NETWORKING: EXPLORING ESSENTIAL PROTOCOLS FOR BEGINNERS

BOOK 2
NAVIGATING NETWORK MANAGEMENT: MASTERING PROTOCOLS FOR EFFICIENT OPERATIONS

BOOK 3
SECURING THE NETWORK: PROTOCOLS, PRACTICES, AND STRATEGIES FOR SAFEGUARDING DATA

BOOK 4
ADVANCED PROTOCOL DYNAMICS: DELVING INTO COMPLEX NETWORK COMMUNICATION STRATEGIES

ROB BOTWRIGHT

Published by Rob Botwright
Library of Congress Cataloging-in-Publication Data
ISBN 978-1-83938-779-1
Cover design by Rizzo

Disclaimer

The contents of this book are based on extensive research and the best available historical sources. However, the author and publisher make no claims, promises, or guarantees about the accuracy, completeness, or adequacy of the information contained herein. The information in this book is provided on an "as is" basis, and the author and publisher disclaim any and all liability for any errors, omissions, or inaccuracies in the information or for any actions taken in reliance on such information. The opinions and views expressed in this book are those of the author and do not necessarily reflect the official policy or position of any organization or individual mentioned in this book. Any reference to specific people, places, or events is intended only to provide historical context and is not intended to defame or malign any group, individual, or entity. The information in this book is intended for educational and entertainment purposes only. It is not intended to be a substitute for professional advice or judgment. Readers are encouraged to conduct their own research and to seek professional advice where appropriate. Every effort has been made to obtain necessary permissions and acknowledgments for all images and other copyrighted material used in this book. Any errors or omissions in this regard are unintentional, and the author and publisher will correct them in future editions.

BOOK 1 - FOUNDATIONS OF NETWORKING: EXPLORING ESSENTIAL PROTOCOLS FOR BEGINNERS

BOOK 2 - NAVIGATING NETWORK MANAGEMENT: MASTERING PROTOCOLS FOR EFFICIENT OPERATIONS

BOOK 3 - SECURING THE NETWORK: PROTOCOLS, PRACTICES, AND STRATEGIES FOR SAFEGUARDING DATA

BOOK 4 - ADVANCED PROTOCOL DYNAMICS: DELVING INTO COMPLEX NETWORK COMMUNICATION STRATEGIES

Introduction

Welcome to the "Network Engineer's Bible," a comprehensive book bundle designed to equip network engineers with the essential knowledge and skills needed to master 100 protocols for communication, management, and security. In today's interconnected world, networks play a crucial role in facilitating communication, managing resources, and ensuring the security of data. Whether you're just starting your journey in networking or seeking to deepen your expertise, this book bundle has something to offer for everyone.

Book 1, "Foundations of Networking," serves as an introduction for beginners, exploring essential protocols that form the building blocks of modern networks. From understanding the basics of TCP/IP to mastering the intricacies of DNS and DHCP, this book provides a solid foundation for aspiring network engineers.

Moving on to Book 2, "Navigating Network Management," we delve into protocols tailored for efficient network operations. From SNMP for monitoring and managing network devices to protocols like SSH and Telnet for remote access, this book empowers network engineers with the tools they need to effectively manage and troubleshoot network infrastructure.

In Book 3, "Securing the Network," we shift our focus to protocols, practices, and strategies for safeguarding data and protecting networks from cyber threats. From encryption protocols like SSL/TLS to security best practices such as access control lists (ACLs) and intrusion detection systems (IDS), this book equips network engineers with the knowledge they need to defend against modern cyber threats.

Finally, in Book 4, "Advanced Protocol Dynamics," we delve into complex network communication strategies, exploring protocols and techniques for optimizing network performance, scalability, and reliability. From advanced routing protocols like OSPF and BGP to innovative approaches like Software-Defined Networking (SDN), this book pushes the boundaries of network engineering, offering insights into cutting-edge technologies and emerging trends.

Together, these four books form a comprehensive guide for network engineers at all levels, providing a roadmap for mastering the diverse landscape of network protocols and advancing their careers in the field of networking. Whether you're a beginner looking to build a strong foundation or an experienced professional seeking to stay ahead of the curve, the "Network Engineer's Bible" is your ultimate companion in the world of networking.

BOOK 1
FOUNDATIONS OF NETWORKING
EXPLORING ESSENTIAL PROTOCOLS FOR BEGINNERS

ROB BOTWRIGHT

Chapter 1: Introduction to Networking Fundamentals

Basics of Network Infrastructure involve understanding the foundational components that enable communication between devices. At the core of any network lies the physical infrastructure, which encompasses the hardware elements such as routers, switches, and cables. Routers play a pivotal role in directing traffic between different networks, facilitating data exchange between devices. A common CLI command to configure a router is 'configure terminal' to enter the global configuration mode, followed by 'interface [interface_name]' to access a specific interface. Within the router configuration, setting IP addresses using the 'ip address [ip_address] [subnet_mask]' command is essential for network connectivity. Switches, on the other hand, function at the data link layer, forwarding data within the same network based on MAC addresses. Configuring VLANs (Virtual Local Area Networks) is a fundamental aspect of switch configuration, achieved through commands like 'vlan [vlan_id]' to create VLANs and 'interface [interface_name]' followed by 'switchport mode access' to assign ports to specific VLANs. Cables, including Ethernet and fiber optic cables, physically connect devices within the network infrastructure, ensuring data transmission between them. Understanding cable types and their appropriate usage is crucial for building a reliable network infrastructure. In addition to physical components, network infrastructure also encompasses logical elements such as IP addressing and subnetting. Proper IP addressing scheme design is vital for efficient data routing and network management. Subnetting, which involves dividing a large network into smaller, more manageable subnetworks, enhances network performance and security. The subnet mask determines the size of each subnet, with common subnetting techniques involving CIDR notation and subnet masks like /24 or /16. Subnetting is often performed using tools like subnet calculators or manually calculated based on network requirements. DHCP (Dynamic Host Configuration Protocol) is another critical aspect of network infrastructure, automating the assignment of IP addresses to devices within a network. DHCP servers dynamically allocate IP addresses, subnet masks, and other configuration parameters to clients, reducing administrative overhead. Configuring a DHCP server involves specifying IP address pools, lease durations, and other parameters through commands like 'ip dhcp pool [pool_name]' in router configuration mode. DNS

(Domain Name System) is a fundamental service in network infrastructure, translating domain names into IP addresses for efficient communication. DNS resolution occurs when a user enters a domain name in a web browser, and the DNS server resolves it to the corresponding IP address. Configuring DNS involves specifying DNS server addresses in device settings or DHCP configurations, ensuring proper name resolution. Security is an integral aspect of network infrastructure, safeguarding data and resources from unauthorized access and malicious threats. Implementing access control lists (ACLs) on routers and switches restricts traffic based on predefined rules, mitigating security risks. ACLs are configured using commands like 'access-list [acl_number] permit/deny [source_address] [wildcard_mask]' in router configuration mode. Firewalls add an additional layer of security by filtering traffic based on port numbers, protocols, and IP addresses, protecting networks from unauthorized access and malicious attacks. Network Address Translation (NAT) is another security measure that hides internal IP addresses from external networks, enhancing network privacy and security. Configuring NAT involves mapping internal private IP addresses to external public IP addresses, typically performed on routers or firewalls. In summary, grasping the basics of network infrastructure is essential for designing, deploying, and maintaining robust and efficient networks. From physical components like routers, switches, and cables to logical elements such as IP addressing, subnetting, DHCP, DNS, and security measures like ACLs, firewalls, and NAT, each aspect plays a crucial role in ensuring seamless communication and data exchange within networks. Continuous learning and understanding of network infrastructure principles empower network administrators to build scalable, secure, and resilient networks that meet the evolving demands of modern connectivity.

Evolution of Networking Technologies traces the development and progression of communication systems from their inception to the present day, illustrating how innovations have shaped the modern digital landscape. The journey begins with the advent of early communication methods, such as smoke signals and carrier pigeons, which laid the groundwork for more sophisticated technologies. As civilizations advanced, so did their methods of communication, leading to the invention of the telegraph in the early 19th century. Samuel Morse's invention revolutionized long-distance communication by enabling messages to be transmitted instantly over electrical wires using Morse code, marking a significant milestone in the evolution of networking. The telegraph paved the way for further innovations, including the telephone, which was patented by Alexander Graham Bell in 1876. The telephone allowed for real-time voice communication over long distances, ushering in an era of interconnectedness and paving the way for future developments in networking. In the mid-20th century, the invention of the computer sparked a new wave of technological advancement, leading to the creation of early computer networks like ARPANET. ARPANET, developed by the United States Department of Defense in the late 1960s, laid the groundwork for the modern internet by establishing the basic principles of packet switching and network protocols. The emergence of TCP/IP (Transmission Control Protocol/Internet Protocol) in the 1970s further standardized communication protocols, enabling diverse computer networks to interconnect and communicate seamlessly. With the commercialization of the internet in the 1990s, networking technologies experienced exponential growth, driven by advancements in hardware, software, and telecommunications infrastructure. The introduction of Ethernet, a widely used networking technology for local area networks (LANs), revolutionized data transmission by providing a standardized method for connecting devices within a network. Ethernet, governed by the IEEE 802.3 standard, remains a cornerstone of modern networking, supporting high-speed data transfer and reliable communication. The evolution of networking technologies also encompasses the development of wireless communication systems, such as Wi-Fi and cellular networks. Wi-Fi, based on the IEEE 802.11 standard, enables wireless connectivity between devices within a local area network, facilitating flexible and convenient access to the internet and other network resources. Deploying Wi-Fi networks involves configuring wireless access points and security settings using commands like 'configure terminal' to access the device's configuration mode and 'interface [interface_name]' to specify wireless interfaces. Cellular networks, on the other hand, enable mobile communication by transmitting data over radio waves between mobile devices and cellular towers. The deployment of cellular networks involves installing and configuring base stations and antennas to provide coverage within a specific geographic area. As networking technologies continue to evolve, the adoption of cloud computing has emerged as a transformative trend, enabling organizations to access and manage computing resources over the internet. Cloud networking leverages virtualization and distributed computing technologies to deliver scalable, on-demand services, such as infrastructure as a service (IaaS), platform as a service (PaaS), and software as a service (SaaS). Deploying cloud-based networking solutions involves configuring virtual networks, security groups, and access controls using cloud management platforms like Amazon Web Services (AWS) or Microsoft Azure. Looking ahead, emerging technologies such as 5G, Internet of Things (IoT), and artificial intelligence (AI) are poised to reshape the future of networking, driving innovation and enabling new possibilities for connectivity and collaboration.

Chapter 2: Understanding the OSI Model: A Framework for Communication

OSI Model Layers and Functions provide a framework for understanding how data is transmitted and processed across networks, encompassing seven distinct layers each with its specific roles and responsibilities. Beginning with the physical layer, it serves as the foundation of the OSI model, responsible for transmitting raw data bits over the physical medium such as copper wires, fiber optic cables, or wireless signals. At this layer, devices like network interface cards (NICs) and switches operate to ensure reliable data transmission by encoding, decoding, and transmitting electrical signals. Configuring physical layer settings involves tasks like setting speed and duplex mode using commands like 'speed [speed_value]' and 'duplex [duplex_mode]' in switch or router interfaces. Moving up the OSI model, the data link layer establishes communication between directly connected devices, encapsulating data into frames and providing error detection and correction mechanisms. Ethernet, a widely used data link layer protocol, governs how devices on the same network communicate, with commands like 'interface

[interface_name]' followed by 'encapsulation dot1q [vlan_id]' used to configure VLAN tagging on switch interfaces. The network layer facilitates end-to-end communication between devices across different networks, routing packets based on logical addresses (IP addresses) and managing network traffic flow. Configuring IP addresses and routes using commands like 'ip address [ip_address] [subnet_mask]' and 'ip route [destination_network] [next_hop]' is essential for network layer operation. The transport layer ensures reliable data delivery by establishing connections, sequencing packets, and performing error recovery and flow control. Transmission Control Protocol (TCP) and User Datagram Protocol (UDP) are common transport layer protocols, each serving distinct communication needs. Configuring TCP parameters like window size and maximum segment size (MSS) using 'tcp window-size [window_size]' and 'tcp mss [mss_value]' commands optimizes transport layer performance. Moving higher in the OSI model, the session layer manages communication sessions between applications, establishing, maintaining, and terminating connections as needed. Session layer protocols facilitate synchronization, checkpointing, and recovery mechanisms to ensure seamless data exchange. The presentation layer is responsible for data translation, encryption, and compression, ensuring that data formats are compatible between communicating devices. Compression techniques like gzip and encryption algorithms like AES are applied at this layer to secure and optimize data transmission. Finally, the application layer provides network services to end-users, facilitating communication between applications and users. Protocols like HTTP, FTP, SMTP, and DNS operate at the application layer, enabling services such as web browsing, file transfer, email communication, and domain name resolution. Understanding the functions of each OSI model layer is essential for network troubleshooting, design, and optimization. By analyzing network traffic and identifying issues at specific layers, network administrators can effectively diagnose and resolve connectivity issues. Additionally, deploying network services and applications requires consideration of the OSI model layers involved, ensuring compatibility and interoperability between different systems and devices. In summary, the OSI model provides a structured approach to network communication, delineating the responsibilities of each layer and facilitating the design, implementation, and maintenance of complex networking infrastructures. As networks continue to evolve, the OSI model remains a foundational framework for understanding and managing network operations. Protocols and Encapsulation in the OSI Model are fundamental concepts that govern the transmission and reception of data across networks, providing a standardized framework for communication between devices. Each layer of the OSI model is associated with specific protocols and encapsulation mechanisms, which define how data is packaged, transmitted, and interpreted at each stage of the communication process. Starting with the physical layer, protocols like Ethernet, Wi-Fi, and Bluetooth define the rules for transmitting raw binary data over the physical medium, whether it's copper cables, fiber optics, or wireless signals. Commands like 'ipconfig' in Windows or 'ifconfig' in Linux are used to display information about network interfaces, including IP addresses, subnet masks, and MAC addresses. As data moves up the OSI model to the data link layer, it is encapsulated into frames, with protocols such as Ethernet, Point-to-Point Protocol (PPP), and IEEE 802.11 (Wi-Fi) governing the framing process. Within Ethernet frames, MAC addresses are used to identify the source and destination devices, facilitating the delivery of data within the same network segment. Configuring Ethernet interfaces on routers and switches involves commands like 'interface [interface_name]' followed by 'encapsulation dot1q [vlan_id]' to specify VLAN tagging for trunk ports. Moving up to the network layer, data is encapsulated into packets, with protocols like

Internet Protocol (IP) providing logical addressing and routing capabilities. IP addresses are assigned to devices to uniquely identify them within a network and facilitate communication between different networks. Routing protocols such as Routing Information Protocol (RIP), Open Shortest Path First (OSPF), and Border Gateway Protocol (BGP) are used to exchange routing information and determine the best path for data transmission. Configuring IP addresses and routes using commands like 'ip address [ip_address] [subnet_mask]' and 'ip route [destination_network] [next_hop]' is essential for network layer operation. As data reaches the transport layer, it is encapsulated into segments, with protocols like Transmission Control Protocol (TCP) and User Datagram Protocol (UDP) providing reliable and connectionless communication, respectively. TCP ensures data delivery by establishing connections, sequencing packets, and performing error recovery and flow control. UDP, on the other hand, offers a lightweight, connectionless alternative suitable for real-time applications like streaming media and online gaming. Configuring TCP and UDP ports using commands like 'access-list [acl_number] permit/deny [protocol] [source_address] [source_port] [destination_address] [destination_port]' is essential for implementing access control and security policies at the transport layer. Moving up to the session layer, data is organized into sessions, with protocols like Secure Shell (SSH), Telnet, and Remote Desktop Protocol (RDP) facilitating communication between network applications. These protocols establish, maintain, and terminate connections between devices, enabling users to remotely access and control systems over the network. Configuring SSH access on routers and switches involves generating cryptographic keys using the 'crypto key generate rsa' command and enabling SSH using the 'ip ssh version [version_number]' command. At the presentation layer, data is formatted and encrypted for transmission, ensuring compatibility between different systems and devices. Compression techniques like gzip and encryption algorithms like Advanced Encryption Standard (AES) are applied to optimize data transmission and enhance security. Finally, at the application layer, data is processed and interpreted by network applications, with protocols like Hypertext Transfer Protocol (HTTP), File Transfer Protocol (FTP), and Simple Mail Transfer Protocol (SMTP) facilitating web browsing, file transfer, and email communication, respectively. Understanding the role of protocols and encapsulation in the OSI model is essential for designing, implementing, and troubleshooting network infrastructures. By adhering to standardized protocols and encapsulation mechanisms, network administrators can ensure interoperability and compatibility between different devices and systems, facilitating seamless communication and data exchange across networks. In summary, protocols and encapsulation are the building blocks of network communication, providing a standardized framework for transmitting, receiving, and interpreting data across the OSI model layers. As networks continue to evolve and expand, adherence to established protocols and encapsulation standards remains crucial for maintaining the reliability, security, and efficiency of modern network infrastructures.

Chapter 3: Unraveling the TCP/IP Protocol Suite

TCP/IP Protocol Architecture forms the foundation of modern internet communication, providing a robust and standardized framework for transmitting data between devices across interconnected networks. The TCP/IP protocol suite consists of a set of protocols organized into four abstraction layers: the Application layer, Transport layer, Internet layer, and Link layer. Beginning with the Application layer, this layer is responsible for providing network services directly to end-users, facilitating communication between applications running on different devices. Protocols such as Hypertext Transfer Protocol (HTTP), File Transfer Protocol (FTP), and Simple Mail Transfer Protocol (SMTP) operate at this layer, enabling web browsing, file transfer, and email communication, respectively. Deploying Application layer protocols involves configuring application-specific settings and parameters, such as server addresses and port numbers, within each application or service. Moving down to the Transport layer, it ensures reliable and efficient data transfer between devices, abstracting the complexities of network communication from higher-layer applications. Transmission Control Protocol (TCP) and User Datagram Protocol (UDP) are the two primary protocols operating at this layer, each serving distinct communication needs. TCP provides reliable, connection-oriented communication by establishing connections, sequencing packets, and performing error recovery and flow control. Configuring TCP parameters like window size and maximum segment size (MSS) using commands like 'tcp window-size [window_size]' and 'tcp mss [mss_value]' optimizes Transport layer performance. On the other hand, UDP offers lightweight, connectionless communication suitable for real-time applications like voice and video streaming. At the Internet layer, IP (Internet Protocol) serves as the cornerstone protocol, providing logical addressing and routing capabilities to enable end-to-end communication across interconnected networks. IP addresses uniquely identify devices within a network and facilitate packet routing based on destination addresses. Configuring IP addresses and routes using commands like 'ip address [ip_address] [subnet_mask]' and 'ip route [destination_network] [next_hop]' is essential for Internet layer operation. Additionally, Internet Control Message Protocol (ICMP) operates at this layer, facilitating network troubleshooting and diagnostic tasks such as ping and traceroute. Moving down to the Link layer, it establishes communication between directly connected devices and encompasses protocols that govern data transmission over local network segments. Ethernet, Wi-Fi, and Bluetooth are common Link layer protocols, each defining rules for framing data into frames and transmitting them over the physical medium. Configuring Link layer protocols involves setting interface parameters like speed, duplex mode, and VLAN tagging using commands like 'interface [interface_name]' followed by 'speed [speed_value]' and 'duplex [duplex_mode]'. The TCP/IP Protocol Architecture's modular design facilitates interoperability and scalability, allowing for the integration of new protocols and technologies as networking requirements evolve. Understanding the role of each layer and its associated protocols is essential for designing, implementing, and troubleshooting TCP/IP-based networks. By adhering to TCP/IP standards and best practices, network administrators can ensure the reliability, security, and performance of their network infrastructures. As networks continue to grow in complexity and scale, adherence to TCP/IP principles remains crucial for maintaining seamless communication and connectivity across diverse environments. In summary, the TCP/IP Protocol Architecture serves as the cornerstone of modern networking, providing a flexible and scalable framework for transmitting data across interconnected networks. By leveraging standardized protocols and layer-based abstraction,

TCP/IP enables efficient communication between devices while abstracting the underlying complexities of network communication. Addressing and Routing in TCP/IP Networks are fundamental concepts that underpin the functionality and efficiency of modern internet communication, enabling devices to locate each other and exchange data across interconnected networks. At the heart of TCP/IP networking lies the Internet Protocol (IP), which provides logical addressing and routing capabilities to facilitate end-to-end communication. IP addresses uniquely identify devices within a network and serve as destinations for data packets, allowing routers to forward packets to their intended destinations. Configuring IP addresses involves assigning unique addresses to each device on a network, typically using the IPv4 or IPv6 addressing scheme. For example, the command 'ip address [ip_address] [subnet_mask]' is used in router configuration mode to assign IP addresses to router interfaces. Subnetting, a technique used to divide a larger network into smaller, more manageable subnetworks, enhances network scalability and efficiency by reducing broadcast domains and optimizing routing. Subnet masks, specified in CIDR notation or dotted decimal format, determine the size and boundaries of each subnet. Routing, the process of forwarding packets from a source to a destination, relies on routing tables maintained by routers to determine the best path for packet delivery. Routing protocols such as Routing Information Protocol (RIP), Open Shortest Path First (OSPF), and Border Gateway Protocol (BGP) are used to exchange routing information and dynamically update routing tables. Configuring static routes using commands like 'ip route [destination_network] [next_hop]' or dynamic routing protocols automates the process of route calculation and propagation, ensuring efficient packet forwarding across networks. IP version 4 (IPv4), the most widely deployed IP protocol, uses 32-bit addresses expressed in dotted decimal notation (e.g., 192.168.1.1), providing approximately 4.3 billion unique addresses. However, with the proliferation of internet-connected devices, the IPv4 address space has become depleted, leading to the adoption of IPv6. IPv6 employs 128-bit addresses, allowing for an exponentially larger address space and enabling the proliferation of internet-connected devices. Migrating to IPv6 involves configuring IPv6 addresses on devices and updating network infrastructure to support IPv6 routing and addressing. For example, the command 'ipv6 address [ipv6_address]/[prefix_length]' is used to assign IPv6 addresses to router interfaces. Additionally, transitioning from IPv4 to IPv6 may require dual-stack configurations to support both address families during the transition period. Network Address Translation (NAT) is another addressing technique used to conserve public IP addresses and enable private network devices to access the internet. NAT translates private IP addresses to a single public IP address when communicating with external networks, allowing multiple devices to share a single public IP address. Configuring NAT involves defining NAT pools, access control lists (ACLs), and translation rules to specify which addresses are translated and how. Virtual Private Networks (VPNs) extend private network connectivity across public networks like the internet, enabling secure communication between geographically dispersed locations. VPNs use tunneling protocols like Point-to-Point Tunneling Protocol (PPTP), Layer 2 Tunneling Protocol (L2TP), and Internet Protocol Security (IPsec) to encapsulate and encrypt data for secure transmission. Deploying VPNs involves configuring VPN endpoints, authentication methods, and encryption algorithms to ensure data confidentiality and integrity. Network administrators use commands like 'crypto isakmp policy' and 'crypto ipsec transform-set' to configure IPsec VPNs on routers and firewalls. In summary, addressing and routing are essential aspects of TCP/IP networking, enabling devices to communicate and exchange data across interconnected networks. By understanding IP addressing, subnetting, routing protocols, and addressing techniques like NAT and VPNs, network administrators can design, deploy, and manage resilient and scalable network infrastructures. As networks continue to evolve and expand, addressing and routing will remain critical components of TCP/IP networking, shaping the future of internet communication.

Chapter 4: Exploring Ethernet and LAN Technologies

Ethernet Standards and Evolution trace the development and standardization of Ethernet technology, which has become the dominant networking technology for local area networks (LANs) and wide area networks (WANs) since its inception in the 1970s. Initially developed by Xerox Corporation's Palo Alto Research Center (PARC) in the early 1970s, Ethernet was designed as a local communication technology for connecting computers and peripherals within a shared environment. Over time, Ethernet evolved from its humble beginnings to become the de facto standard for wired networking, with various standards bodies, including the Institute of Electrical and Electronics Engineers (IEEE), playing a crucial role in its standardization and advancement. The IEEE 802.3 standard, commonly known as Ethernet, defines the physical and data link layer specifications for Ethernet networks, including frame formats, signaling methods, and media access control (MAC) protocols. The original Ethernet standard, known as 10BASE5, operated at a data rate of 10 Mbps (megabits per second) over thick coaxial cable, using a bus topology with vampire taps for device connections. Subsequent Ethernet standards, such as 10BASE2 and 10BASE-T, introduced improvements in cable type and connectivity, including thin coaxial cable (10BASE2) and twisted-pair copper cabling (10BASE-T). Configuring Ethernet interfaces on routers and switches involves setting parameters like speed and duplex mode using commands like 'speed [speed_value]' and 'duplex [duplex_mode]' in interface configuration mode. The evolution of Ethernet continued with the introduction of Fast Ethernet (IEEE 802.3u) in the early 1990s, which increased data rates to 100 Mbps and introduced full-duplex communication for improved performance. Fast Ethernet enabled organizations to achieve higher throughput and lower latency in LAN environments, facilitating the adoption of bandwidth-intensive applications like multimedia streaming and file sharing. Gigabit Ethernet (IEEE 802.3ab) further pushed the boundaries of Ethernet performance, delivering data rates of up to 1 Gbps (gigabit per second) over twisted-pair copper cabling and optical fiber. Gigabit Ethernet became the standard for high-speed LAN connectivity, offering ten times the performance of Fast Ethernet and laying the groundwork for future advancements in network speed and capacity. Commands like 'interface [interface_name]' followed by 'speed auto' and 'duplex auto' are used to enable auto-negotiation on Ethernet interfaces, allowing devices to automatically determine the optimal speed and duplex settings for communication. The evolution of Ethernet continued with the introduction of 10 Gigabit Ethernet (IEEE 802.3ae), which increased data rates to 10 Gbps and expanded Ethernet's reach to high-performance computing, data center interconnects, and metropolitan area networks (MANs). 10 Gigabit Ethernet operates over various media types, including copper twisted-pair, multimode fiber optic, and single-mode fiber optic cables, providing flexibility and scalability for different networking environments. Deploying 10 Gigabit Ethernet requires configuring compatible network interfaces, switches, and cabling infrastructure to support the higher data rates and transmission distances associated with 10 Gbps networking. In recent years, Ethernet speeds have continued to increase with the development of 25 Gigabit Ethernet, 40 Gigabit Ethernet, and 100 Gigabit Ethernet standards, catering to the growing demands of cloud computing, big data analytics, and high-performance networking applications. Configuring advanced Ethernet features like VLANs (Virtual Local Area Networks) and link aggregation involves commands like 'vlan [vlan_id]' to create VLANs and 'channel-group [channel_number] mode [mode]' to configure port channels for link aggregation. As Ethernet technology evolves, standardization bodies like the IEEE continue to drive innovation and define new standards to meet the ever-increasing demands of modern networking. In summary, Ethernet standards have undergone significant evolution since their inception, from the original 10 Mbps Ethernet to the multi-gigabit speeds of today's Ethernet networks. By adhering to standardized Ethernet specifications and leveraging advanced features and technologies, organizations can build scalable, high-performance Ethernet infrastructures to meet their networking needs now and in the future.

LAN Technologies and Topologies encompass a variety of networking technologies and physical arrangements that enable communication and data exchange within local area networks (LANs), serving as the foundation for modern network infrastructures. Ethernet, the most prevalent LAN technology, defines the standards and protocols for wired networking, facilitating the transmission of data packets over copper or fiber optic cables.

Configuring Ethernet interfaces on routers and switches involves setting parameters like speed and duplex mode using commands like 'speed [speed_value]' and 'duplex [duplex_mode]' in interface configuration mode. Ethernet operates at the data link layer of the OSI model and uses the Carrier Sense Multiple Access with Collision Detection (CSMA/CD) media access control method to manage access to the network medium and avoid collisions. The introduction of Fast Ethernet and Gigabit Ethernet standards increased data rates to 100 Mbps and 1 Gbps, respectively, enabling higher throughput and supporting bandwidth-intensive applications. Configuring Ethernet interfaces for higher speeds involves deploying compatible network interface cards (NICs) and switches that support the desired Ethernet standard, ensuring compatibility and optimal performance. In addition to Ethernet, wireless LAN (Wi-Fi) technologies provide flexible connectivity for mobile devices and wireless access points (APs), enabling wireless communication within LAN environments. Wi-Fi operates over radio frequencies and utilizes the IEEE 802.11 standard to define protocols and specifications for wireless networking. Configuring Wi-Fi access points involves setting parameters such as SSID (Service Set Identifier), security settings, and channel assignments to ensure reliable wireless connectivity. Wireless LAN technologies support various standards, including 802.11a, 802.11b, 802.11g, 802.11n, 802.11ac, and 802.11ax (Wi-Fi 6), each offering different data rates, frequency bands, and modulation schemes. Deploying wireless LANs requires careful planning to optimize coverage, minimize interference, and ensure security, with commands like 'ssid [ssid_name]' and 'encryption [encryption_type]' used to configure Wi-Fi access point settings. LAN topologies define the physical or logical layout of network devices and the connections between them, influencing network performance, scalability, and fault tolerance. Common LAN topologies include bus, star, ring, mesh, and hybrid topologies, each with its advantages and disadvantages. In a bus topology, all devices are connected to a single communication medium, with data transmitted sequentially from one device to another. Configuring devices in a bus topology involves connecting them to a shared communication channel, such as coaxial cable or Ethernet bus, and ensuring proper termination to prevent signal reflections. A star topology features a central network device, such as a switch or hub, to which all other devices connect individually, forming a centralized point of communication. Configuring a star topology involves connecting devices to the central switch or hub using twisted-pair copper cables or fiber optic cables and configuring switch ports for proper operation. In a ring topology, devices are connected in a closed loop, with data transmitted sequentially around the ring from one device to the next until it reaches its destination. Configuring devices in a ring topology involves connecting them in a physical or logical ring configuration and implementing mechanisms like token passing or frame forwarding to manage data transmission. Mesh topologies provide redundant paths between devices, enhancing fault tolerance and reliability by allowing data to traverse multiple routes. Configuring devices in a mesh topology involves establishing direct connections between devices and implementing routing protocols to manage traffic and optimize path selection. Hybrid topologies combine two or more basic topologies to meet specific networking requirements, such as combining star and mesh topologies to create a hybrid mesh topology with centralized control and redundant paths. Deploying hybrid topologies involves configuring devices according to the characteristics of each topology component and ensuring seamless integration between them. In summary, LAN technologies and topologies form the building blocks of local area networks, providing the infrastructure and connectivity required for efficient communication and data exchange. By understanding the characteristics and capabilities of different LAN technologies and topologies, network administrators can design, deploy, and manage LAN environments that meet the needs of their organizations while ensuring reliability, scalability, and performance.

Chapter 5: Discovering the World of Wireless Protocols

Wireless Networking Standards encompass a diverse range of specifications and protocols that govern wireless communication and connectivity, enabling devices to transmit and receive data over radio frequencies without physical cables. The Institute of Electrical and Electronics Engineers (IEEE) plays a central role in standardizing wireless networking technologies through its 802.11 family of standards, commonly known as Wi-Fi. Configuring Wi-Fi access points involves setting parameters such as SSID (Service Set Identifier), security settings, and channel assignments to ensure reliable wireless connectivity. The original IEEE 802.11 standard, released in 1997, defined the groundwork for wireless LAN (WLAN) communication, operating in the 2.4 GHz frequency band and supporting data rates of up to 2 Mbps. Commands like 'ssid [ssid_name]' and 'encryption [encryption_type]' are used to configure Wi-Fi access point settings. Subsequent amendments to the IEEE 802.11 standard introduced enhancements in data rates, security, and frequency bands, expanding the capabilities and reach of wireless networking. The IEEE 802.11a standard, released in 1999, introduced operation in the 5 GHz frequency band and supported data rates of up to 54 Mbps, providing improved performance and reduced interference compared to 802.11b. Deploying wireless LANs requires careful planning to optimize coverage, minimize interference, and ensure security. The IEEE 802.11b standard, also released in 1999, operated in the 2.4 GHz frequency band and supported data rates of up to 11 Mbps, offering backward compatibility with existing 802.11 devices. Configuring wireless LANs involves configuring compatible network interfaces, switches, and cabling infrastructure to support the desired wireless standards and data rates. The IEEE 802.11g standard, released in 2003, combined the best aspects of 802.11a and 802.11b by operating in the 2.4 GHz frequency band and supporting data rates of up to 54 Mbps, providing backward compatibility with 802.11b devices and improved performance over longer ranges. Configuring devices in a wireless LAN involves setting parameters such as SSID (Service Set Identifier), security settings, and channel assignments to ensure reliable connectivity. The IEEE 802.11n standard, released in 2009, introduced significant improvements in data rates, range, and reliability by employing multiple-input multiple-output (MIMO) technology, spatial multiplexing, and channel bonding. Commands like 'ssid [ssid_name]' and 'encryption [encryption_type]' are used to configure Wi-Fi access point settings. The IEEE 802.11ac standard, released in 2013, further advanced wireless networking by increasing data rates and channel widths, operating in the 5 GHz frequency band, and supporting multi-user MIMO (MU-MIMO) for simultaneous communication with multiple devices. Deploying wireless LANs requires careful planning to optimize coverage, minimize interference, and ensure security. The IEEE 802.11ax standard, also known as Wi-Fi 6, represents the latest evolution in wireless networking technology, introducing enhancements in data rates, capacity, and efficiency to meet the growing demands of modern wireless networks. Configuring wireless LANs involves configuring compatible network interfaces, switches, and cabling infrastructure to support the desired wireless standards and data rates. In summary, wireless networking standards have evolved over the years, from the original IEEE 802.11 standard to the latest Wi-Fi 6 standard, offering increasingly faster data rates, greater range, and improved reliability. By adhering to standardized wireless specifications and leveraging advanced features and technologies, organizations can build resilient, high-performance wireless networks to meet their connectivity needs now and in the future.

Wireless Security and Authentication Mechanisms are essential components of wireless networking, designed to protect against unauthorized access, data interception, and network intrusions in wireless environments. Securing wireless networks involves implementing encryption, authentication, and access control mechanisms to safeguard data confidentiality, integrity, and availability. Configuring Wi-Fi access points involves setting parameters such as SSID (Service Set Identifier), security settings, and channel assignments to ensure reliable wireless connectivity. One of the fundamental security measures in wireless networks is encryption, which encodes transmitted data to prevent unauthorized users from intercepting and deciphering sensitive information. The Wi-Fi Protected Access (WPA) protocol, introduced as an interim security solution, addressed vulnerabilities in the original Wired Equivalent Privacy (WEP) standard by implementing stronger encryption algorithms and dynamic key exchange mechanisms. Commands like 'ssid [ssid_name]' and 'encryption [encryption_type]' are used to configure Wi-Fi access point settings. However, with advances in computing power and cryptographic attacks, WPA became susceptible to security vulnerabilities, prompting the development of the more robust WPA2 standard. WPA2 employs the Advanced Encryption Standard (AES) encryption algorithm and the Counter Mode with Cipher Block Chaining Message Authentication Code Protocol (CCMP) for data confidentiality and integrity, providing stronger protection against attacks. Deploying wireless LANs requires careful planning to optimize coverage, minimize interference, and ensure security. To further enhance security, Wi-Fi Protected Access 3 (WPA3) was introduced, offering improved encryption protocols, enhanced security for open networks, and stronger protection against brute-force attacks. Configuring devices in a wireless LAN involves setting parameters such as SSID (Service Set Identifier), security settings, and channel assignments to ensure reliable connectivity. WPA3 also introduces individualized data encryption for each wireless client, protecting data transmitted between devices from eavesdropping and interception. In addition to encryption, authentication mechanisms play a crucial role in verifying the identity of users and devices attempting to access a wireless network. The Extensible Authentication Protocol (EAP) framework provides a flexible framework for implementing various authentication methods in wireless networks. The IEEE 802.1X standard defines port-based network access control, requiring users or devices to authenticate themselves before gaining access to the network. Configuring wireless LANs involves configuring compatible network interfaces, switches, and cabling infrastructure to support the desired wireless standards and data rates. EAP methods such as EAP-TLS (Transport Layer Security), EAP-TTLS (Tunneled Transport Layer Security), and PEAP (Protected Extensible Authentication Protocol) facilitate secure authentication using digital certificates, username/password credentials, or other authentication mechanisms. Deploying wireless LANs requires careful planning to optimize coverage, minimize interference, and ensure security. Another authentication mechanism commonly used in wireless networks is pre-shared key (PSK) authentication, where users or devices authenticate themselves using a shared passphrase or key. While PSK authentication is convenient for small-scale deployments, it may be susceptible to brute-force attacks if weak passwords are used. Configuring wireless LANs involves configuring compatible network interfaces, switches, and cabling infrastructure to support the desired wireless standards and data rates. To mitigate security risks, it is essential to use strong, complex passwords and regularly update them to prevent unauthorized access. In summary, wireless security and authentication mechanisms are critical for protecting wireless networks from unauthorized access, data breaches, and security threats. By implementing robust encryption, authentication, and access control measures, organizations can ensure the confidentiality, integrity, and availability of their wireless communications while minimizing the risk of security incidents and breaches.

Chapter 6: Navigating Internet Protocol (IP) Addressing

IP Address Types and Classes encompass a diverse range of address formats and classifications used to identify devices and networks in the Internet Protocol (IP) networking architecture, facilitating communication and data exchange across interconnected networks. The Internet Protocol version 4 (IPv4) addresses are the most widely used addressing scheme in IP networks, employing a 32-bit address space divided into four octets separated by periods, with each octet representing a decimal value ranging from 0 to 255. Configuring IP addresses involves assigning unique addresses to each device on a network, typically using the IPv4 or IPv6 addressing scheme. IPv4 addresses are categorized into five classes: Class A, Class B, Class C, Class D, and Class E, based on the leading bits of the address and the network size they support. Class A addresses use the first octet to identify the network portion of the address, with the remaining three octets reserved for host addresses, enabling large-scale networks to accommodate a vast number of devices. Commands like 'ip address [ip_address] [subnet_mask]' are used in router configuration mode to assign IP addresses to router interfaces. Class B addresses designate the first two octets for network identification and the remaining two octets for host addresses, making them suitable for medium-sized networks with moderate numbers of devices. Class C addresses allocate the first three octets for network identification and the final octet for host addresses, making them ideal for small-scale networks with limited numbers of devices. Class D addresses are reserved for multicast communication, allowing devices to subscribe to and receive data sent to multicast groups, with addresses in the range of 224.0.0.0 to 239.255.255.255. Class E addresses are reserved for experimental and research purposes, with addresses in the range of 240.0.0.0 to 255.255.255.255, and are not intended for general use in IP networks. IPv6, the successor to IPv4, employs a 128-bit address space represented in hexadecimal format, allowing for an exponentially larger number of unique addresses compared to IPv4. Configuring IPv6 addresses involves setting IPv6 addresses on devices and updating network infrastructure to support IPv6 routing and addressing. IPv6 addresses are categorized into several types, including unicast, multicast, and anycast addresses, each serving distinct communication requirements. Unicast addresses identify a single network interface on a device and enable point-to-point communication between devices, with commands like 'ipv6 address [ipv6_address]/[prefix_length]' used to assign IPv6 addresses to router interfaces. Multicast addresses facilitate one-to-many communication by enabling a single sender to transmit data to multiple recipients simultaneously, with addresses in the range of ff00::/8 reserved for multicast use. Anycast addresses represent multiple devices that share the same address, allowing packets to be routed to the nearest device in a group, improving efficiency and reliability. IPv6 also introduces link-local and global unicast addresses, with link-local addresses used for communication within a single subnet and global unicast addresses used for communication across different networks. Deploying IPv6 involves configuring IPv6 addresses on devices, enabling IPv6 routing protocols, and updating network infrastructure to support IPv6 connectivity. In summary, IP address types and classes play a crucial role in identifying devices and networks in IP networking, facilitating communication and data exchange across interconnected networks. By understanding the characteristics and classifications of IP addresses, network administrators can design, deploy, and manage IP networks that meet the connectivity needs of their organizations while ensuring scalability, efficiency, and security. Subnetting and CIDR Notation are fundamental concepts in IP networking, allowing network administrators to efficiently allocate and manage IP addresses within a network infrastructure, thus maximizing address utilization and optimizing routing efficiency. Subnetting involves dividing a larger network into smaller, more manageable subnetworks, or subnets, to improve network performance, security, and scalability. The subnet mask, represented in binary format, determines the size and boundaries of each subnet, enabling devices to identify network and host portions of IP addresses. Configuring subnet masks involves specifying the number of network bits and host bits in the subnet mask, using commands like 'subnet-mask [subnet_mask]' in router interface configuration mode to define subnet masks for router interfaces. CIDR (Classless Inter-Domain Routing) notation is a compact representation of IP addresses and subnet masks, expressed in the form of IP address followed by a forward slash and a subnet mask length, such as 192.168.1.0/24, where the subnet mask length indicates the number of network bits. CIDR notation facilitates efficient addressing and routing by simplifying the representation of IP address ranges and subnet sizes, reducing overhead and complexity in network configurations. Calculating the number of subnets and hosts in a subnet involves applying subnetting techniques and understanding binary arithmetic to determine the network and host portions of IP addresses. For example, a subnet mask of /24 indicates that the first 24 bits are allocated for network identification, leaving 8 bits for host addresses, resulting in 256 possible subnets and 254 usable host addresses per subnet. Subnetting allows organizations to segment networks based on geographic location, department, or function, enhancing network security and management by isolating traffic and controlling access between subnets. Deploying subnetting involves designing a subnetting scheme that aligns with the organization's network requirements and growth projections, allocating IP address ranges and subnet masks to each subnet, and updating network devices to reflect the new subnetting configuration. VLSM (Variable Length Subnet Masking) is an advanced subnetting technique that allows for the creation of subnets with different sizes within the same network, optimizing address utilization and accommodating varying numbers of hosts in different subnets. Configuring VLSM involves assigning subnet masks of different lengths to subnets based on the number of hosts required, using commands like 'ip address [ip_address] [subnet_mask]' in router interface configuration mode to assign IP addresses to router interfaces. Subnetting and CIDR notation also play a crucial role in routing and summarization, enabling routers to efficiently forward packets between subnets and aggregate routing information to reduce the size of routing tables. Route summarization, also known as route aggregation, involves combining multiple smaller IP address ranges into a single larger address range, reducing the number of routing table entries and simplifying routing decisions. Configuring route summarization involves defining summary routes for contiguous IP address ranges, using commands like 'ip route [network_address] [subnet_mask] [next_hop]' in router configuration mode to create summary routes and specify next-hop routers for forwarding traffic. Summarized routes improve routing efficiency and scalability by reducing the size of routing updates and minimizing the memory and processing requirements on routers. In summary, subnetting and CIDR notation are essential techniques in IP networking, allowing organizations to optimize address utilization, improve network performance, and enhance routing efficiency. By understanding and implementing subnetting and CIDR notation effectively, network administrators can design, deploy, and manage IP networks that meet the connectivity needs of their organizations while ensuring scalability, flexibility, and security.

Chapter 7: Demystifying Domain Name System (DNS)

DNS Resolution Process is a fundamental aspect of the Domain Name System (DNS), facilitating the translation of domain names into IP addresses, thus enabling communication between devices on the internet. The DNS resolution process begins when a user enters a domain name, such as www.example.com, into a web browser or application, initiating a DNS query to resolve the domain name to an IP address. The first step in the DNS resolution process involves the client device sending a DNS query to a recursive resolver, typically provided by the user's Internet Service Provider (ISP) or configured in the network settings. The DNS query contains the domain name that the client wants to resolve and is sent over the User Datagram Protocol (UDP) or Transmission Control Protocol (TCP) to port 53, the standard DNS port. Using commands like 'nslookup' or 'dig' in the command-line interface (CLI), users can perform DNS queries to resolve domain names and retrieve corresponding IP addresses. The recursive resolver receives the DNS query and checks its cache to see if it has the

IP address corresponding to the requested domain name stored locally. If the IP address is found in the cache and is still valid, the resolver returns the IP address to the client, completing the DNS resolution process. However, if the IP address is not found in the cache or has expired, the resolver acts as a client itself and sends a recursive query to the DNS root servers to start the resolution process. The DNS root servers are a crucial component of the DNS infrastructure, providing information about the authoritative name servers responsible for top-level domains (TLDs) such as .com, .org, and .net. The root servers respond to the recursive resolver's query with a referral to the authoritative name servers responsible for the appropriate TLD, such as the .com TLD servers for the domain www.example.com. The recursive resolver then sends another query to the TLD servers, requesting the IP address of the domain name's authoritative name server. The TLD servers respond with a referral to the authoritative name server for the specific domain, which is responsible for maintaining the DNS records for that domain. The recursive resolver sends a final query to the authoritative name server, requesting the IP address corresponding to the original domain name. The authoritative name server responds with the IP address, which is then returned to the client by the recursive resolver, completing the DNS resolution process. Throughout the DNS resolution process, various DNS resource records, including A records, AAAA records, CNAME records, and NS records, are used to map domain names to IP addresses and identify authoritative name servers. A records map domain names to IPv4 addresses, while AAAA records map domain names to IPv6 addresses. CNAME records provide aliases for domain names, allowing multiple domain names to point to the same IP address, while NS records specify the authoritative name servers for a domain. Deploying and managing DNS servers involves configuring DNS zones, records, and server settings to ensure reliable and efficient DNS resolution for client devices. Administrators can use CLI commands like 'dig', 'nslookup', 'host', or 'ping' to troubleshoot DNS issues, perform DNS lookups, and verify DNS resolution. Monitoring DNS traffic and server performance using tools like Wireshark or DNS query log analysis can help identify and resolve DNS-related issues, ensuring optimal performance and reliability of DNS resolution processes. In summary, the DNS resolution process is a critical component of internet communication, enabling users to access websites, send emails, and connect to online services by translating domain names into IP addresses. By understanding the DNS resolution process and deploying effective DNS infrastructure, organizations can ensure fast, reliable, and secure access to internet resources for their users. DNS Record Types and Their Functions encompass a variety of resource records used in the Domain Name System (DNS) to map domain names to IP addresses, identify authoritative name servers, and facilitate internet communication. A records, also known as address records, are one of the most common DNS record types and are used to map domain names to IPv4 addresses. Using the 'nslookup' command in the command-line interface (CLI), users can query DNS servers to retrieve A records for specific domain names, providing the corresponding IPv4 addresses. AAAA records, also known as quad-A records, perform a similar function to A records but map domain names to IPv6 addresses, enabling communication over IPv6 networks. By querying DNS servers using the 'nslookup' or 'dig' command, users can retrieve AAAA records for domain names and obtain the corresponding IPv6 addresses. CNAME records, or canonical name records, provide aliases for domain names, allowing multiple domain names to point to the same IP address. When a CNAME record is queried using the 'nslookup' or 'dig' command, the DNS server returns the canonical name associated with the alias, redirecting clients to the original domain name. MX records, or mail exchange records, specify the mail servers responsible for receiving email messages for a domain. By querying DNS servers for MX records using the 'nslookup' or 'dig' command, email clients can determine the mail servers to which email messages should be delivered for a specific domain. PTR records, or pointer records, perform reverse DNS lookups by mapping IP addresses to domain names. When queried using the 'nslookup' or 'dig' command with the '-x' option, PTR records provide the domain names associated with IPv4 or IPv6 addresses, enabling identification of the corresponding hosts. NS records, or name server records, identify the authoritative name servers responsible for a domain. By querying DNS servers for NS records using the 'nslookup' or 'dig' command, clients can determine the authoritative name servers for a specific domain, facilitating DNS resolution and delegation of authority. TXT records, or text records, store arbitrary text data associated with a domain. TXT records are commonly used for domain verification, email authentication, and other purposes, with clients querying DNS servers for TXT records using the 'nslookup' or 'dig' command to retrieve the text data associated with a domain. SOA records, or start of authority records, provide essential information about a DNS zone, including the primary name server, email address of the zone administrator, serial number, refresh interval, retry interval, expiry interval, and minimum TTL (time to live). By querying DNS servers for SOA records using the 'nslookup' or 'dig' command, administrators can obtain important details about DNS zones and their configuration. SRV records, or service records, specify the location of services within a domain, such as SIP, LDAP, or XMPP services. When queried using the 'nslookup' or 'dig' command, SRV records provide the hostname, port number, priority, and weight of the service, enabling clients to locate and connect to services on the network. Deploying DNS record types involves configuring DNS zones, records, and server settings to ensure accurate and efficient DNS resolution for client devices. Administrators can use CLI commands like 'dig', 'nslookup', 'host', or 'ping' to query DNS servers, troubleshoot DNS issues, and verify DNS record configurations. Monitoring DNS traffic and server performance using tools like Wireshark or DNS query log analysis can help identify and resolve DNS-related issues, ensuring optimal performance and reliability of DNS services. In summary, DNS record types play a crucial role in the Domain Name System, facilitating the translation of domain names to IP addresses, identification of authoritative name servers, and routing of internet traffic. By understanding the functions and deployment of DNS record types, administrators can configure and manage DNS infrastructure to ensure fast, reliable, and secure access to internet resources for users and applications.

Chapter 8: Introduction to Routing and Routing Protocols

Routing Basics and Concepts are fundamental principles in networking, governing the process of forwarding data packets between devices on interconnected networks, facilitating communication and data exchange. Routing involves determining the optimal path for packet transmission based on destination IP addresses, network topology, and routing protocols. The 'route' command in the command-line interface (CLI) allows users to view and manipulate routing tables on routers and switches, providing insights into the routing decisions made by network devices. One of the key concepts in routing is the routing table, a data structure stored in memory on routers and switches that contains information about network destinations and the next-hop routers for packet forwarding. By querying routing tables using the 'route' command, administrators can identify the routes configured on network devices and troubleshoot routing issues. Routing protocols are algorithms and protocols used by routers to exchange routing information and dynamically update routing tables, ensuring efficient packet delivery in changing network conditions. Common routing protocols include RIP (Routing Information Protocol), OSPF (Open Shortest Path First), EIGRP (Enhanced Interior Gateway Routing Protocol), and BGP (Border Gateway Protocol). Using the 'show ip route' or 'show ip ospf neighbor' command in the CLI, administrators can monitor routing protocol operation and view routing information exchanged between routers. Static routing is a routing technique where network administrators manually configure routing tables on routers, specifying static routes for destination networks and next-hop routers. Static routes are typically used in small-scale networks or for specific routing requirements, providing simplicity and predictability in routing configurations. The 'ip route' command in the CLI allows administrators to configure static routes on routers, specifying destination networks, subnet masks, and next-hop IP addresses. Dynamic routing, on the other hand, is a routing technique where routers exchange routing information using routing protocols to dynamically update routing tables and adapt to network changes. Dynamic routing protocols use algorithms to calculate the best path to destination networks based on factors such as hop count, bandwidth, and network delay. Administrators can configure dynamic routing protocols using commands like 'router rip', 'router ospf', 'router eigrp', or 'router bgp' in the CLI, specifying protocol parameters and network advertisements. Interior Gateway Protocols (IGPs) are routing protocols used within autonomous systems to exchange routing information between routers. IGPs include RIP, OSPF, and EIGRP, and are designed for use within a single organization's network infrastructure. Exterior Gateway Protocols (EGPs), such as BGP, are routing protocols used between autonomous systems to exchange routing information between different organizations' networks. BGP is widely used in internet routing to facilitate communication between autonomous systems and ensure global connectivity. Routing metrics are criteria used by routing algorithms to determine the best path to destination networks. Common routing metrics include hop count, bandwidth, delay, reliability, and cost. By configuring routing metrics using commands like 'bandwidth', 'delay', or 'cost' in the CLI, administrators can influence routing decisions and optimize network performance. Route aggregation, also known as route summarization, is a routing technique where multiple smaller IP address ranges are combined into a single larger address range, reducing the size of routing tables and improving routing efficiency. Administrators can configure route aggregation using commands like 'ip summary-address' or 'aggregate-address' in the CLI, specifying address ranges and mask lengths to summarize routes. Route redistribution is the process of exchanging routing information between different routing domains or protocols, allowing routers to learn about routes from multiple sources. Administrators can configure route redistribution using commands like 'redistribute' in the CLI, specifying the source and destination routing protocols and filtering criteria. Monitoring and troubleshooting routing involves analyzing routing tables, routing protocol operation, and routing protocol messages to identify and resolve routing issues. Administrators can use CLI commands like 'show ip route', 'show ip ospf interface', or 'debug ip routing' to monitor routing information and diagnose routing problems. In summary, routing basics and concepts are essential components of network design and operation, enabling routers to forward data packets between devices and networks efficiently. By understanding routing principles and deploying routing techniques effectively, administrators can build scalable, resilient, and high-performance networks that meet the connectivity needs of organizations and users. Distance Vector vs. Link State Routing Protocols are two distinct categories of routing protocols used in computer networks, each employing different algorithms and mechanisms to exchange routing information and calculate optimal paths to destination networks. Distance Vector Routing Protocols, such as RIP (Routing Information

Protocol) and RIPv2, determine the best path to destination networks based on hop count, where each router forwards routing updates to neighboring routers at regular intervals. The 'show ip route' command in the command-line interface (CLI) allows administrators to view the routing table on routers running distance vector routing protocols, providing insights into the routes learned and the next-hop routers for packet forwarding. Distance Vector Routing Protocols use the Bellman-Ford algorithm or its variations to calculate the shortest path to destination networks, with routers periodically exchanging routing updates containing information about known networks and their associated costs. By configuring parameters like routing timers and administrative distances, administrators can influence the behavior and convergence speed of distance vector routing protocols. One of the limitations of distance vector routing protocols is their susceptibility to routing loops and slow convergence in large networks, where changes in network topology may take time to propagate and converge. Link State Routing Protocols, such as OSPF (Open Shortest Path First) and IS-IS (Intermediate System to Intermediate System), operate by exchanging link state advertisements (LSAs) between routers to build a complete map of the network topology. The 'show ip ospf database' command in the CLI allows administrators to view the OSPF link state database on routers, containing information about routers, links, and network segments in the OSPF domain. Link State Routing Protocols use the Dijkstra algorithm to calculate the shortest path to destination networks, considering factors such as link costs and network bandwidth. By dividing networks into areas and summarizing routing information between areas, administrators can scale OSPF deployments and optimize network convergence. Link State Routing Protocols offer faster convergence and greater scalability than distance vector routing protocols, making them well-suited for large enterprise networks and service provider environments. OSPF supports features such as hierarchical design, route summarization, and authentication, providing flexibility and robustness in network deployments. IS-IS, another link state routing protocol, is widely used in internet service provider (ISP) networks and telecommunications networks, offering fast convergence and efficient link utilization. When deploying link state routing protocols, administrators must consider factors such as network topology, link bandwidth, and convergence requirements to design optimal routing configurations. By configuring OSPF areas, router priorities, and interface costs, administrators can control routing behavior and optimize network performance. Link state routing protocols use flooding mechanisms to propagate link state advertisements (LSAs) throughout the network, ensuring that all routers have consistent and up-to-date information about network topology. However, flooding can cause excessive network traffic and overhead in large networks, requiring careful design and optimization. OSPF supports features such as hierarchical design, route summarization, and authentication, providing flexibility and robustness in network deployments. IS-IS, another link state routing protocol, is widely used in internet service provider (ISP) networks and telecommunications networks, offering fast convergence and efficient link utilization. When deploying link state routing protocols, administrators must consider factors such as network topology, link bandwidth, and convergence requirements to design optimal routing configurations. By configuring OSPF areas, router priorities, and interface costs, administrators can control routing behavior and optimize network performance. Link state routing protocols use flooding mechanisms to propagate link state advertisements (LSAs) throughout the network, ensuring that all routers have consistent and up-to-date information about network topology. However, flooding can cause excessive network traffic and overhead in large networks, requiring careful design and optimization. In summary, Distance Vector and Link State Routing Protocols are two categories of routing protocols with distinct characteristics and mechanisms for exchanging routing information and calculating optimal paths in computer networks. By understanding the differences between these protocols and deploying them effectively, administrators can build scalable, resilient, and high-performance networks that meet the connectivity needs of organizations and users.

Chapter 9: Embracing Transmission Control Protocol (TCP)

TCP Handshake and Connection Establishment are fundamental processes in the Transmission Control Protocol (TCP), governing how devices establish communication sessions and exchange data packets reliably across networks. The TCP handshake is a three-way process that occurs between a client and a server to establish a TCP connection, ensuring both parties are synchronized and ready to exchange data. To initiate the TCP handshake, the client sends a SYN (synchronize) packet to the server, indicating its intention to establish a connection. Using the 'tcpdump' command in the command-line interface (CLI), administrators can capture network traffic and analyze TCP handshake packets to troubleshoot connectivity issues and monitor network activity. Upon receiving the SYN packet, the server responds with a SYN-ACK (synchronize-acknowledgment) packet, acknowledging the client's request and indicating its readiness to establish a connection. The 'netstat' command allows administrators to view active TCP connections on servers and clients, providing insights into established connections, listening ports, and connection states. Finally, the client sends an ACK (acknowledgment) packet to the server, confirming the receipt of the SYN-ACK packet and completing the TCP handshake process. By examining TCP header fields such as sequence numbers, acknowledgment numbers, and flags, administrators can analyze TCP handshake packets and diagnose network issues. TCP connections are identified by a tuple of source IP address, source port, destination IP address, and destination port, known as the 4-tuple, ensuring unique identification of communication sessions between devices. TCP connections can be either half-open, where one party has sent a SYN packet but has not yet received an ACK, or fully established, where both parties have completed the TCP handshake process. TCP connections are bidirectional, allowing data to be transmitted in both directions between the client and server. During data transmission, TCP segments are encapsulated with sequence numbers and acknowledgment numbers to ensure reliable delivery and orderly data exchange. The 'tcpdump' command allows administrators to capture and analyze TCP segments exchanged between devices, providing insights into packet loss, retransmissions, and network performance. TCP employs mechanisms such as flow control, congestion control, and error recovery to optimize data transmission and mitigate network congestion and packet loss. Flow control mechanisms, such as the sliding window algorithm, regulate the flow of data between sender and receiver to prevent buffer overflow and optimize bandwidth utilization. Congestion control mechanisms, such as TCP's slow start and congestion avoidance algorithms, dynamically adjust the transmission rate based on network conditions to prevent congestion and maintain network stability. Error recovery mechanisms, such as TCP's selective acknowledgment (SACK) and fast retransmit algorithms, detect and retransmit lost or corrupted segments to ensure reliable data delivery. By monitoring TCP header fields such as sequence numbers, acknowledgment numbers, and window sizes, administrators can analyze TCP segments and identify performance issues, packet loss, and network congestion. TCP connections can be terminated either gracefully or abruptly, depending on the application's requirements and the reason for termination. In a graceful termination, both the client and server exchange FIN (finish) packets to close the connection gracefully, indicating their intention to end the communication session. The 'tcpdump' command allows administrators to capture and analyze TCP termination packets, providing insights into connection closure and network behavior. In an abrupt termination, one party may send a RST (reset) packet to forcibly close the connection, indicating an error condition or abnormal termination. By monitoring network traffic and analyzing TCP header fields, administrators can troubleshoot connection termination issues and ensure proper closure of TCP connections. In summary, TCP handshake and connection establishment are essential processes in TCP/IP networking, ensuring reliable communication and data exchange between devices. By understanding the TCP handshake process, connection states, and data transmission mechanisms, administrators can optimize network performance, troubleshoot connectivity issues, and ensure the reliability of TCP connections in computer networks.

TCP Congestion Control Algorithms play a crucial role in regulating data transmission rates and ensuring network stability in TCP/IP networking, where congestion occurs when network resources become overwhelmed with data traffic, leading to packet loss, delays, and degraded performance. One of the earliest congestion control algorithms developed for TCP is Slow Start, which dynamically adjusts the size of the congestion window (cwnd) based on network conditions and available bandwidth. Slow Start gradually increases the cwnd size exponentially until it reaches a threshold known as the slow start threshold (ssthresh), at which point it transitions to the congestion avoidance phase. Administrators can monitor TCP congestion control algorithms and their parameters using network performance monitoring tools such as Wireshark or tcpdump, which capture and analyze TCP segments exchanged between devices, providing insights into congestion window sizes, packet loss events, and retransmissions. Another congestion control algorithm used in TCP is Congestion Avoidance, which regulates the growth of the congestion window more conservatively by increasing it linearly rather than exponentially, thereby reducing the likelihood of network congestion. By analyzing TCP header fields such as sequence numbers, acknowledgment numbers, and window sizes, administrators can evaluate the effectiveness of congestion control algorithms and identify performance issues, packet loss events, and network congestion. TCP also employs mechanisms such as Fast Retransmit and Fast Recovery to recover from packet loss events and minimize the impact of congestion on data transmission. Fast Retransmit detects packet loss based on duplicate acknowledgments received from the receiver and triggers the retransmission of the missing segment without waiting for a timeout to occur. Fast Recovery maintains the sending rate of TCP connections during packet loss events by halving the congestion window size and entering a congestion avoidance phase, allowing the sender to recover quickly from congestion without drastic reductions in throughput. By monitoring TCP header fields such as sequence numbers, acknowledgment numbers, and window sizes, administrators can analyze TCP segments and detect packet loss events, triggering fast retransmit and fast recovery mechanisms to ensure reliable data delivery. TCP congestion control algorithms are continuously evolving to adapt to changing network conditions and improve performance in modern networking environments. Variants of TCP, such as TCP Cubic and TCP Vegas, introduce enhancements to congestion control algorithms to optimize throughput, minimize latency, and improve fairness in network resource allocation. TCP Cubic, for example, adjusts the congestion window more aggressively during slow start and congestion avoidance phases, leading to faster ramp-up of data transmission rates and improved network utilization. TCP Vegas, on the other hand, uses an estimation of the round-trip time (RTT) to predict network congestion before it occurs, allowing it to reduce the transmission rate preemptively to prevent congestion and minimize packet loss. By deploying modern TCP congestion control algorithms and monitoring network performance using tools like Wireshark or tcpdump, administrators can optimize TCP/IP networking, ensure reliable data transmission, and mitigate the impact of network congestion on application performance. In summary, TCP congestion control algorithms are essential mechanisms in TCP/IP networking, regulating data transmission rates and ensuring network stability in the face of congestion. By understanding the principles of congestion control and deploying effective algorithms, administrators can optimize network performance, improve reliability, and enhance the user experience in computer networks.

Chapter 10: Secure Communication with Secure Sockets Layer (SSL) and Transport Layer Security (TLS)

SSL/TLS Protocol Overview is essential for securing data transmission over computer networks, providing encryption, authentication, and data integrity mechanisms to protect sensitive information from unauthorized access and interception. SSL (Secure Sockets Layer) and its successor TLS (Transport Layer Security) are cryptographic protocols that establish secure communication channels between clients and servers, enabling secure data exchange over the internet. SSL/TLS protocols use a combination of symmetric and asymmetric encryption algorithms to encrypt data transmitted between endpoints, ensuring confidentiality and privacy. Administrators can configure SSL/TLS protocols on web servers using server software such as Apache or Nginx, enabling HTTPS (HTTP Secure) communication and encrypting data exchanged between web browsers and servers. One of the key components of SSL/TLS protocols is the SSL/TLS handshake, a process that occurs at the beginning of a communication session to establish cryptographic parameters and authenticate the parties involved. During the

SSL/TLS handshake, the client and server exchange cryptographic keys, negotiate encryption algorithms, and verify each other's identities using digital certificates issued by trusted certificate authorities (CAs). Administrators can generate SSL/TLS certificates for web servers using certificate management tools such as OpenSSL or Let's Encrypt, obtaining certificates signed by trusted CAs to validate the authenticity of their servers. SSL/TLS protocols support various encryption algorithms and cipher suites, including RSA, DSA, Diffie-Hellman, AES, and ChaCha20, allowing administrators to configure strong encryption for secure communication. By analyzing SSL/TLS handshake packets using network protocol analyzers like Wireshark, administrators can inspect cryptographic parameters, certificate chains, and encryption algorithms negotiated during the handshake process, ensuring the security of SSL/TLS connections. SSL/TLS protocols also provide mechanisms for server authentication, where servers present digital certificates to clients to prove their identities and establish trust. Clients verify the authenticity of server certificates by validating their digital signatures and checking certificate chains against trusted root certificates installed on client devices. Administrators can deploy SSL/TLS protocols on email servers, FTP servers, and other network services to encrypt data transmission and protect sensitive information from eavesdropping and tampering. SSL/TLS protocols have evolved over time to address security vulnerabilities and support modern cryptographic algorithms and protocols. TLS 1.2 and TLS 1.3 are the latest versions of the TLS protocol, offering improved security, performance, and compatibility with legacy systems. Administrators can configure web servers to prioritize TLS 1.2 and TLS 1.3 connections over older versions of SSL/TLS to ensure the highest level of security for encrypted communication. SSL/TLS protocols also include mechanisms for session resumption, where clients and servers can reuse previously established cryptographic parameters to expedite the SSL/TLS handshake process and reduce connection latency. By enabling session resumption techniques such as session tickets or session IDs, administrators can optimize SSL/TLS performance and enhance user experience on web servers. SSL/TLS protocols play a crucial role in securing online transactions, protecting sensitive data such as credit card numbers, passwords, and personal information exchanged between clients and servers. E-commerce websites, online banking platforms, and social media networks rely on SSL/TLS encryption to safeguard user privacy and prevent data breaches. Administrators can configure SSL/TLS protocols to enforce security best practices such as Perfect

Forward Secrecy (PFS), which ensures that session keys are not compromised even if long-term private keys are compromised. By implementing SSL/TLS protocols with PFS support, administrators can enhance the security of encrypted communication and mitigate the risk of data exposure in the event of a security breach. In summary, SSL/TLS protocols are essential components of secure communication on the internet, providing encryption, authentication, and data integrity mechanisms to protect sensitive information from unauthorized access and interception. By deploying SSL/TLS protocols and adhering to security best practices, administrators can ensure the confidentiality, integrity, and authenticity of data transmitted over computer networks. SSL/TLS Certificates and Handshake Process are integral components of secure communication on the internet, enabling encryption, authentication, and data integrity mechanisms to protect sensitive information from unauthorized access and interception. SSL/TLS certificates, also known as digital certificates, are cryptographic files that bind the identity of a website or server to a cryptographic key, providing assurance to clients that they are communicating with a legitimate entity. Administrators can obtain SSL/TLS certificates from trusted certificate authorities (CAs) such as Let's Encrypt, DigiCert, or Comodo, by submitting certificate signing requests (CSRs) generated on web servers using tools like OpenSSL or Certbot. The 'openssl req' command allows administrators to generate CSRs and private keys for SSL/TLS certificates, specifying certificate attributes such as common name, organization name, and country code. Once issued by the CA, SSL/TLS certificates are installed on web servers and configured to enable HTTPS (HTTP Secure) communication, encrypting data exchanged between web browsers and servers. The SSL/TLS handshake process occurs at the beginning of a communication session between a client and server to establish cryptographic parameters and authenticate the parties involved. During the handshake, the client sends a ClientHello message to the server, indicating its support for SSL/TLS protocols and cryptographic algorithms. The server responds with a ServerHello message, selecting the highest version of SSL/TLS supported by both parties and negotiating encryption algorithms and cipher suites for secure communication. Administrators can configure SSL/TLS protocols and cipher suites on web servers to prioritize strong encryption algorithms such as AES (Advanced Encryption Standard) and elliptic curve cryptography (ECC), ensuring the security of SSL/TLS connections. Following the ServerHello message, the server sends its SSL/TLS certificate to the client, along with additional information such as the server's public key and supported cipher suites. The client verifies the authenticity of the server's certificate by checking its digital signature and validating the certificate chain against trusted root certificates installed on the client device. Administrators can use tools like OpenSSL or online SSL/TLS validation services to inspect SSL/TLS certificates, verify certificate chains, and identify potential security vulnerabilities. Once the client has validated the server's certificate, it generates a pre-master secret and encrypts it with the server's public key, sending the encrypted pre-master secret to the server in a ClientKeyExchange message. The server decrypts the pre-master secret using its private key and uses it to derive session keys for symmetric encryption of data transmitted between the client and server. Administrators can monitor SSL/TLS handshake messages using network protocol analyzers like Wireshark or tcpdump, capturing and analyzing handshake packets to troubleshoot SSL/TLS configuration issues and diagnose security vulnerabilities. After successfully exchanging cryptographic parameters and establishing session keys, the client and server exchange Finished messages to confirm the completion of the SSL/TLS handshake process. The encrypted session keys derived during the handshake are used to encrypt and decrypt data transmitted between the client and server, ensuring confidentiality and integrity of communication. Administrators can configure SSL/TLS protocols to enforce Perfect Forward Secrecy (PFS), a security feature that ensures that session keys are ephemeral and not derived from long-term private keys, preventing retroactive decryption of intercepted data. By enabling PFS support in SSL/TLS configurations, administrators can enhance the security of encrypted communication and protect against potential security threats. In summary, SSL/TLS certificates and the handshake process are essential mechanisms for establishing secure communication on the internet, providing encryption, authentication, and data integrity mechanisms to protect sensitive information from unauthorized access and interception. By deploying SSL/TLS certificates and configuring SSL/TLS protocols effectively, administrators can ensure the confidentiality, integrity, and authenticity of data transmitted over computer networks.

BOOK 2

NAVIGATING NETWORK MANAGEMENT

MASTERING PROTOCOLS FOR EFFICIENT OPERATIONS*ROB BOTWRIGHT*

Chapter 1: Introduction to Network Management

The Role and Importance of Network Management in modern computer networks cannot be overstated, as it encompasses a wide range of tasks and responsibilities essential for ensuring the efficient operation, security, and performance of network infrastructure. Network management involves the administration, monitoring, and maintenance of network devices, services, and protocols to meet organizational goals and user requirements. Administrators can use network management tools such as SNMP (Simple Network Management Protocol) to monitor and manage network devices, gathering information about device status, performance metrics, and configuration settings. The 'snmpwalk' command allows administrators to retrieve SNMP data from network devices, querying SNMP agents to obtain information such as system uptime, interface status, and CPU utilization. By analyzing SNMP data using network monitoring platforms like Nagios or Zabbix, administrators can identify performance bottlenecks, troubleshoot connectivity issues, and optimize network performance. Network management encompasses various tasks, including device configuration, fault detection and resolution, performance monitoring, security management, and compliance auditing. Administrators can use configuration management tools like Ansible or Puppet to automate device provisioning and configuration, ensuring consistency and compliance with organizational policies. The 'ansible-playbook' command allows administrators to deploy configuration changes across multiple network devices simultaneously, reducing manual errors and improving operational efficiency. Fault management is another critical aspect of network management, involving the detection, isolation, and resolution of network faults to minimize downtime and service disruptions. Network monitoring tools like SolarWinds or PRTG enable administrators to monitor network devices and services in real-time, alerting them to potential issues such as device failures, link outages, or excessive bandwidth utilization. By configuring alerting thresholds and notifications, administrators can proactively address network faults before they escalate into service outages or performance degradation. Performance management is essential for optimizing network performance and ensuring the efficient utilization of network resources. Administrators can use performance monitoring tools like Grafana or Prometheus to collect and analyze performance metrics such as throughput, latency, and packet loss, identifying areas for improvement and capacity planning. By visualizing performance data through dashboards and reports, administrators can gain insights into network behavior and trends, enabling informed decision-making and resource allocation. Security management is a critical aspect of network management, involving the implementation of security policies, access controls, and threat mitigation strategies to protect network assets from unauthorized access, data breaches, and cyber attacks. Administrators can use security management tools like firewalls, intrusion detection systems (IDS), and security information and event management (SIEM) platforms to monitor network traffic, detect anomalies, and enforce security policies. By analyzing security logs and audit trails, administrators can identify security incidents, investigate root causes, and implement remediation measures to strengthen network defenses. Compliance auditing is essential for ensuring adherence to regulatory requirements, industry standards, and internal policies governing network security and operations. Administrators can use compliance management tools like Nessus or OpenSCAP to assess network security posture, conduct vulnerability scans, and generate compliance reports. By remediating security vulnerabilities and addressing audit findings, administrators can demonstrate compliance with regulatory mandates and mitigate legal and financial risks. In summary, the role and importance of network management in modern computer networks are paramount, encompassing various tasks and responsibilities essential for ensuring the efficient operation, security, and performance of network infrastructure. By leveraging network management tools and best practices, administrators can monitor and manage network devices, detect and resolve faults, optimize performance, enforce security policies, and demonstrate compliance with regulatory requirements.

Components of Network Management Systems (NMS) play a crucial role in overseeing the operation, monitoring, and maintenance of computer networks, encompassing various hardware, software, and processes designed to facilitate efficient network administration and optimization. One of the key components of an NMS is the Network Management Station (NMS), a centralized management platform that serves as the control center for network administrators to monitor and manage network devices, services, and performance. Administrators can deploy NMS software such as Nagios, Zabbix, or SolarWinds to configure network monitoring and management tasks, providing a unified interface for monitoring network health, detecting faults, and analyzing performance metrics. By installing NMS software on dedicated servers or virtual machines, administrators can access centralized dashboards and reports, enabling them to oversee network operations and troubleshoot issues effectively. Another essential component of NMS is the Managed Devices, which comprise network devices such as routers, switches, firewalls, servers, and endpoints that are monitored and managed by the NMS. Administrators can use protocols like SNMP (Simple Network Management Protocol) to communicate with managed devices, collecting information about device status, configuration settings, and performance metrics. The 'snmpwalk' command allows administrators to query SNMP agents on managed devices, retrieving information such as system uptime, interface statistics, and CPU utilization. By configuring SNMP agents on network devices and defining SNMP communities or access control lists (ACLs), administrators can grant NMS access to managed devices and enforce security policies to protect sensitive information. Network Monitoring Tools are essential components of NMS, providing features such as real-time monitoring, alerting, reporting, and trend analysis to help administrators detect and respond to network issues promptly. Monitoring tools like PRTG, Cacti, or Observium enable administrators to monitor network traffic, device availability, bandwidth utilization, and application performance, generating alerts and notifications when predefined thresholds are exceeded. By configuring monitoring thresholds and notification policies, administrators can proactively address network issues and minimize downtime, ensuring the reliability and availability of network services. Event Management is another critical component of NMS, involving the collection, correlation, and analysis of event data generated by network devices and services. Event management tools like Splunk, ELK Stack (Elasticsearch, Logstash, Kibana), or Graylog enable administrators to centralize event logs, parse log data, and identify patterns or anomalies indicative of security incidents or performance issues. By configuring event correlation rules and alerts, administrators can automate incident response processes and prioritize remediation efforts based on the severity and impact of events. Configuration Management is essential for maintaining consistency and compliance across network devices and services, ensuring that configuration settings are standardized and aligned with organizational policies. Configuration management tools like Ansible, Puppet, or Chef enable administrators to automate device provisioning, configuration changes, and software updates, reducing manual errors and improving operational efficiency. By defining configuration templates and policies, administrators can enforce configuration standards and track changes to network configurations over time, facilitating auditing and troubleshooting activities. Performance Management is a critical component of NMS, involving the monitoring and optimization of network performance to meet service level agreements (SLAs) and user expectations. Performance management tools like Grafana, Prometheus, or PRTG enable administrators to collect and analyze performance metrics such as throughput, latency, packet loss, and jitter, identifying performance bottlenecks and optimizing resource allocation. By visualizing performance data through dashboards and reports, administrators can gain insights into network behavior and trends, enabling informed decision-making and capacity planning. Security Management is paramount for protecting network assets from unauthorized access, data breaches, and cyber attacks, encompassing tasks such as access control, threat detection, and vulnerability management. Security management tools like firewalls, intrusion detection systems (IDS), and vulnerability scanners enable administrators to enforce security policies, monitor network traffic, and assess the security posture of network devices and services. By configuring firewall rules, implementing network segmentation, and conducting regular security assessments, administrators can mitigate security risks and ensure compliance with regulatory requirements. Compliance Management is essential for demonstrating adherence to regulatory mandates, industry standards, and internal policies governing network security and operations. Compliance management tools like Nessus, OpenSCAP, or Qualys enable administrators to conduct vulnerability scans, assess security controls, and generate compliance reports. By remediating security vulnerabilities and addressing audit findings, administrators can demonstrate compliance with regulatory requirements and mitigate legal and financial risks. In summary, the components of Network Management Systems (NMS) are essential for overseeing the operation, monitoring, and maintenance of computer networks, providing administrators with the tools and capabilities needed to ensure the reliability, security, and performance of network infrastructure. By deploying NMS software, configuring monitoring and management tasks, and leveraging automation and analytics capabilities, administrators can proactively detect and respond to network issues, optimize resource utilization, and mitigate security risks effectively.

Chapter 2: Understanding Simple Network Management Protocol (SNMP)

SNMP (Simple Network Management Protocol) Architecture and Components form the backbone of network management systems, providing a standardized framework for monitoring and managing network devices and services. SNMP is comprised of several key components, including managed devices, agents, managers, and Management Information Bases (MIBs), each playing a vital role in the SNMP architecture. Managed devices are network devices such as routers, switches, firewalls, servers, and printers that are capable of being monitored and managed using SNMP. These devices contain SNMP agents, which are software modules responsible for collecting and reporting management information to SNMP managers. SNMP agents communicate with SNMP managers using SNMP messages, exchanging data in a structured format defined by the SNMP protocol. Administrators can configure SNMP agents on managed devices to enable SNMP monitoring and management, specifying parameters such as community strings and access control lists (ACLs) to control access to SNMP data. The 'snmp-server' command on Cisco routers and switches allows administrators to configure SNMP settings, including SNMP version, community strings, and SNMP trap destinations. SNMP managers are central control points in the SNMP architecture, responsible for monitoring and managing managed devices using SNMP. These managers collect management information from SNMP agents, analyze performance metrics, and generate alerts or notifications based on predefined thresholds. SNMP managers can be standalone applications or integrated into network management platforms, providing a unified interface for administrators to monitor and control network devices. The 'snmpwalk' command is used by SNMP managers to retrieve SNMP data from managed devices, performing a series of SNMP GETNEXT requests to traverse the SNMP tree and retrieve information from SNMP-enabled objects. Management Information Bases (MIBs) are structured databases that contain definitions of managed objects, representing various aspects of network devices and services. MIBs define the hierarchy of SNMP objects and their associated attributes, providing a standardized framework for accessing and managing management information. SNMP managers use MIBs to interpret SNMP data received from managed devices, mapping SNMP object identifiers (OIDs) to human-readable names and values. Standard MIBs such as SNMPv2-MIB and IF-MIB define commonly used objects and attributes for managing network devices, while vendor-specific MIBs extend the functionality of SNMP to support proprietary features and capabilities. Administrators can use MIB browsers or SNMP management tools to browse MIBs, view object definitions, and access SNMP data using OID-based queries. The 'snmpget' command allows administrators to retrieve specific SNMP variables from managed devices, specifying the OID of the desired object and the SNMP community string for authentication. SNMP Trap Notifications are asynchronous messages sent by SNMP agents to SNMP managers to alert them to significant events or conditions occurring on managed devices. These traps provide real-time notifications of events such as link up/down, interface errors, device reboots, or CPU utilization exceeding a threshold. Administrators can configure SNMP traps on managed devices to send trap notifications to designated SNMP managers, enabling proactive monitoring and alerting of network issues. The 'snmp-server enable traps' command is used to enable SNMP traps on Cisco devices, specifying the type of traps to be generated and the destination SNMP manager. SNMP Versions dictate the capabilities and security features supported by SNMP, with SNMPv1, SNMPv2c, and SNMPv3 being the most widely used versions. SNMPv1 is the original version of SNMP and provides basic functionality for monitoring and managing network devices, but lacks strong authentication and encryption mechanisms, making it vulnerable to security threats. SNMPv2c introduces improvements such as support for bulk data retrieval and SNMP community-based security, but still lacks robust security features. SNMPv3 is the most secure version of SNMP, offering authentication, encryption, and access control mechanisms to protect SNMP communication and data integrity. Administrators can configure SNMPv3 settings on managed devices and SNMP managers to enable secure communication using features such as SNMPv3 user authentication and encryption. In summary, SNMP Architecture and Components form the foundation of network management systems, providing a standardized framework for monitoring and managing network devices and services. By understanding the role of managed devices, agents, managers, MIBs, SNMP messages, and SNMP versions, administrators can deploy SNMP-based solutions effectively, enabling proactive monitoring, efficient management, and secure communication in computer networks. SNMP (Simple Network Management Protocol) Versions and Features are essential components of network management systems, offering different capabilities and security mechanisms to monitor and manage network devices and services effectively. SNMP has evolved over time, with three main versions commonly used in network environments: SNMPv1, SNMPv2c, and SNMPv3, each introducing improvements and enhancements to address the changing requirements of network management. SNMPv1, the original version of SNMP, provides basic functionality for monitoring and managing network devices, allowing administrators to retrieve and modify management information using simple GET, SET, and GETNEXT operations. However, SNMPv1 lacks strong security features, relying solely on community strings for authentication, which are transmitted in clear text, making them susceptible to eavesdropping and unauthorized access. Administrators can configure SNMPv1 settings on managed devices and SNMP managers using CLI commands such as 'snmp-server community' on Cisco devices, specifying the community string and access permissions for SNMP operations. SNMPv2c (Community-based SNMPv2) improves upon SNMPv1 by introducing features such as bulk data retrieval and SNMP community-based security, enhancing scalability and efficiency for managing large networks. SNMPv2c allows administrators to retrieve multiple pieces of data in a single request using GETBULK operations, reducing network overhead and improving performance. However, SNMPv2c still lacks robust security mechanisms, relying on community strings for authentication and access control, which are susceptible to security threats such as unauthorized access and data manipulation. Administrators can configure SNMPv2c settings on managed devices and SNMP managers using CLI commands similar to SNMPv1, specifying the community string and access permissions for SNMP operations. SNMPv3 is the most secure version of SNMP, offering authentication, encryption, and access control mechanisms to protect SNMP communication and data integrity. SNMPv3 introduces features such as user-based security model (USM) and view-based access control model (VACM), providing fine-grained control over SNMP operations and access permissions. Administrators can configure SNMPv3 settings on managed devices and SNMP managers using CLI commands such as 'snmp-server user' on Cisco devices, specifying the security level, authentication method, and encryption algorithm for SNMP communication. SNMPv3 supports multiple authentication and encryption algorithms, including MD5, SHA, DES, and AES, allowing administrators to choose the appropriate security mechanisms based on their security requirements and compliance mandates. One of the key features of SNMPv3 is its ability to provide message integrity, ensuring that SNMP messages have not been tampered with during transmission. This is achieved through the use of cryptographic hash functions such as MD5 or SHA, which generate message digests that are appended to SNMP messages and verified by the receiving SNMP entity. Administrators can configure SNMPv3 authentication settings using CLI commands such as 'snmp-server user auth' on Cisco devices, specifying the authentication method and passphrase for message authentication. SNMPv3 also provides data confidentiality through message encryption, ensuring that SNMP data is protected from eavesdropping and interception. This is achieved through the use of symmetric encryption algorithms such as DES or AES, which encrypt SNMP messages before transmission and decrypt them upon receipt. Administrators can configure SNMPv3 encryption settings using CLI commands such as 'snmp-server user priv' on Cisco devices, specifying the encryption method and passphrase for message encryption. SNMPv3 access control features allow administrators to define access policies and restrictions for SNMP operations, ensuring that only authorized users and applications can access and modify management information. Administrators can configure SNMPv3 access control settings using CLI commands such as 'snmp-server group' and 'snmp-server view' on Cisco devices, specifying the group membership and MIB views for SNMP users. In summary, SNMP Versions and Features provide administrators with a range of options for monitoring and managing network devices and services, from basic functionality in SNMPv1 to enhanced security and scalability in SNMPv3. By understanding the capabilities and limitations of each SNMP version, administrators can deploy SNMP-based solutions effectively, ensuring the reliability, security, and performance of network management operations.

Chapter 3: Configuring and Monitoring Devices with SNMP

SNMP Configuration on Network Devices is a fundamental aspect of network management, enabling administrators to monitor and manage devices efficiently using the Simple Network Management Protocol (SNMP), a standard protocol for network monitoring and management. Configuring SNMP involves several steps, including enabling SNMP services, defining community strings, configuring access control, and specifying SNMP versions and parameters. The first step in SNMP configuration is to enable SNMP services on the network device, allowing it to respond to SNMP queries and transmit SNMP traps to SNMP managers. This can be done using CLI commands such as 'snmp-server' on Cisco devices, which enables the SNMP agent and specifies the SNMP version to use. Once SNMP services are enabled, administrators need to define community strings, which are used for authentication and access control in SNMP communication. Community strings act as passwords that grant access to SNMP data and operations, and administrators can configure them using CLI commands such as 'snmp-server community' on Cisco devices, specifying the community string and access permissions. It's essential to choose strong community strings and avoid using default or common strings to enhance security and prevent unauthorized access. Access control is another critical aspect of SNMP configuration, allowing administrators to restrict access to SNMP data and operations based on IP addresses, SNMP versions, and community strings. Administrators can configure access control using CLI commands such as 'snmp-server view' and 'snmp-server group' on Cisco devices, specifying the IP address range, MIB view, and access permissions for SNMP users. By defining access control policies, administrators can ensure that only authorized users and applications can access and modify SNMP data. SNMP versions and parameters must also be configured to ensure compatibility and security in SNMP communication. Administrators can specify SNMP versions (e.g., SNMPv1, SNMPv2c, SNMPv3) and parameters such as authentication method, encryption algorithm, and message integrity using CLI commands such as 'snmp-server user' on Cisco devices. SNMPv3 is the most secure version of SNMP and provides authentication, encryption, and access control mechanisms to protect SNMP communication and data integrity. Once SNMP configuration is complete, administrators can verify the configuration and test SNMP functionality using CLI commands such as 'show snmp' on Cisco devices, which displays SNMP settings and status information. Administrators can also use SNMP management tools such as SNMP MIB browsers or SNMP monitoring platforms to query SNMP-enabled devices, retrieve management information, and monitor SNMP traps. SNMP configuration should be periodically reviewed and updated to ensure compliance with security policies and address changing network requirements. Administrators should regularly audit SNMP settings, community strings, and access control policies to identify and mitigate security risks such as unauthorized access, data breaches, and SNMP-based attacks. By following best practices and guidelines for SNMP configuration, administrators can ensure the reliability, security, and performance of network management operations, enabling proactive monitoring, efficient troubleshooting, and effective resource management. In summary, SNMP Configuration on Network Devices is a crucial task for network administrators, enabling them to monitor and manage devices effectively using SNMP. By following a systematic approach to SNMP configuration and implementing security best practices, administrators can enhance the reliability, security, and efficiency of network management operations, ensuring the smooth operation of the network infrastructure.

SNMP Monitoring Tools and Techniques are essential components of network management, providing administrators with the means to monitor and manage network devices effectively using the Simple Network Management Protocol (SNMP), a standard protocol for network monitoring and management. SNMP monitoring tools enable administrators to collect and analyze management information from SNMP-enabled devices, monitor network performance, detect faults, and troubleshoot issues proactively. These tools offer a range of features and capabilities, including real-time monitoring, historical data analysis, alerting, reporting, and automation, to help administrators optimize network performance and ensure the reliability and availability of network services. One of the key features of SNMP monitoring tools is real-time monitoring, which allows administrators to monitor network devices and services in real-time, providing visibility into device status, performance metrics, and traffic patterns. Real-time monitoring tools such as PRTG Network Monitor, SolarWinds Network Performance Monitor, and Nagios XI enable administrators to view live data streams, track device uptime and availability, and identify performance anomalies as they occur. By monitoring network devices in real-time, administrators can detect and respond to issues promptly, minimizing downtime and service disruptions. Historical data analysis is another important feature of SNMP monitoring tools, allowing administrators to analyze historical performance data to identify trends, patterns, and potential issues. Historical data analysis tools such as Cacti, Zabbix, and Grafana enable administrators to collect, store, and visualize historical performance data, facilitating trend analysis, capacity planning, and troubleshooting. By analyzing historical performance data, administrators can identify performance bottlenecks, predict future resource requirements, and optimize network performance proactively. Alerting is a critical capability of SNMP monitoring tools, enabling administrators to receive notifications and alerts when predefined thresholds are exceeded or specific events occur. Alerting tools such as ManageEngine OpManager, Splunk, and Datadog allow administrators to configure alerting rules based on performance metrics, device status, and event triggers, sending notifications via email, SMS, or other channels. By configuring alerting rules, administrators can be notified of critical issues in real-time, enabling them to take immediate action to resolve problems and minimize the impact on network operations. Reporting is another essential feature of SNMP monitoring tools, enabling administrators to generate customized reports and dashboards to visualize network performance, track key performance indicators (KPIs), and demonstrate compliance with service level agreements (SLAs). Reporting tools such as Observium, LibreNMS, and PRTG Network Monitor enable administrators to generate reports on device availability, bandwidth utilization, error rates, and other performance metrics, providing insights into network performance and trends. By generating reports and dashboards, administrators can communicate network performance metrics effectively to stakeholders, identify areas for improvement, and make data-driven decisions to optimize network operations. Automation is becoming increasingly important in SNMP monitoring tools, enabling administrators to automate routine tasks, streamline workflows, and improve operational efficiency. Automation tools such as Ansible,

Puppet, and Chef allow administrators to automate device provisioning, configuration management, and troubleshooting tasks, reducing manual errors and accelerating problem resolution. By automating repetitive tasks, administrators can free up time for strategic initiatives, improve productivity, and enhance the overall reliability of network operations. Integration is another key aspect of SNMP monitoring tools, allowing administrators to integrate SNMP data with other monitoring and management systems to create a unified view of network performance and health. Integration tools such as Grafana, Elasticsearch, and Logstash enable administrators to aggregate SNMP data with data from other sources such as syslog, NetFlow, and application logs, providing a comprehensive view of network performance and enabling correlation and analysis of disparate data sources. By integrating SNMP data with other monitoring systems, administrators can gain deeper insights into network behavior, identify root causes of performance issues, and optimize resource allocation effectively. In summary, SNMP Monitoring Tools and Techniques are essential for effective network management, providing administrators with the means to monitor and manage network devices, services, and performance metrics efficiently. By leveraging the features and capabilities of SNMP monitoring tools, administrators can gain visibility into network performance, detect and respond to issues proactively, and optimize network operations to ensure the reliability and availability of network services.

Chapter 4: Exploring Remote Monitoring (RMON) Protocols

RMON (Remote Monitoring) Overview and Functionality are crucial aspects of network management, providing administrators with enhanced capabilities for monitoring and analyzing network traffic and performance remotely. RMON is an extension of SNMP (Simple Network Management Protocol) and offers advanced features and functionalities for monitoring network devices and services. RMON enables administrators to monitor network traffic, detect performance issues, and troubleshoot problems effectively, without the need for manual intervention. The primary function of RMON is to collect and analyze network traffic data from remote devices, such as routers, switches, and firewalls, using SNMP. RMON agents installed on these devices capture network traffic data and generate RMON statistics and reports, which can be accessed and analyzed by RMON management stations. The RMON architecture consists of two main components: RMON probes and RMON management stations. RMON probes are software modules installed on network devices, responsible for collecting and analyzing network traffic data. RMON probes capture traffic data at various levels of the OSI (Open Systems Interconnection) model, including network layer (Layer 3) and application layer (Layer 7), providing detailed insights into network behavior and performance. RMON probes support different types of data collection methods, such as packet capture, flow-based sampling, and statistical analysis, allowing administrators to monitor network traffic comprehensively. RMON management stations are software applications or appliances that retrieve and analyze RMON data collected by RMON probes. RMON management stations provide a user-friendly interface for administrators to view RMON statistics, generate reports, and perform troubleshooting tasks. RMON management stations support various features, such as real-time monitoring, historical data analysis, alerting, and reporting, enabling administrators to monitor network performance proactively and identify potential issues before they affect network operations. One of the key benefits of RMON is its ability to monitor network traffic at the granular level, providing detailed insights into network utilization, bandwidth consumption, and application performance. RMON statistics include metrics such as packet counts, byte counts, error rates, and protocol distribution, allowing administrators to identify traffic patterns, pinpoint bottlenecks, and optimize network resources effectively. By analyzing RMON statistics, administrators can detect abnormal behavior, such as network congestion or malicious activity, and take appropriate actions to mitigate risks and ensure the integrity and availability of network services. RMON also supports alarm and event management, allowing administrators to configure threshold-based alerts and notifications for critical network events. Administrators can define thresholds for specific performance metrics, such as bandwidth utilization, error rates, or packet loss, and configure RMON probes to generate alerts when these thresholds are exceeded. Alerts can be sent to administrators via email, SNMP traps, or other notification mechanisms, enabling them to respond to network issues promptly and minimize downtime. RMON reports provide valuable insights into network performance and behavior, enabling administrators to assess the effectiveness of network policies, identify areas for improvement, and make informed decisions to optimize network operations. RMON reports include summaries, trend analysis, and historical data, allowing administrators to track key performance indicators (KPIs), measure the impact of network changes, and demonstrate compliance with service level agreements (SLAs). By generating RMON reports regularly, administrators can gain visibility into network trends, identify potential issues, and implement proactive measures to enhance network performance and reliability. RMON is an essential tool for network troubleshooting, providing administrators with the means to diagnose and resolve network issues quickly and efficiently. RMON probes capture detailed traffic data, including packet captures and protocol decodes, allowing administrators to analyze network traffic at the packet level and identify the root cause of performance problems. Administrators can use RMON data to troubleshoot network issues such as bandwidth congestion, packet loss, latency, and network errors, and implement corrective actions to restore normal network operation. By leveraging RMON for troubleshooting, administrators can reduce mean time to repair (MTTR), minimize service disruptions, and improve overall network reliability and availability. In summary, RMON Overview and Functionality play a vital role in network management, providing administrators with powerful capabilities for monitoring, analyzing, and troubleshooting network traffic and performance. By deploying RMON probes and management stations, administrators can gain visibility into network behavior, detect performance issues, and optimize network resources effectively, ensuring the reliability and availability of network services.

RMON (Remote Monitoring) Alarm and Event Management are critical components of network management, providing administrators with the ability to monitor network devices and services for predefined conditions and events, and generate alerts and notifications when these conditions are met. RMON alarm and event management allow administrators to detect and respond to network issues proactively, minimizing downtime and service disruptions. RMON supports various types of alarms and events, including threshold-based alarms, event-based alarms, and combination alarms, allowing administrators to configure alerts based on specific performance metrics, device status, or network events. Threshold-based alarms are triggered when predefined thresholds for performance metrics, such as bandwidth utilization, error rates, or packet loss, are exceeded. Administrators can configure threshold-based alarms using RMON management stations, specifying the performance metric, threshold value, and action to be taken when the threshold is exceeded. For example, administrators can configure an alarm to alert them via email or SNMP trap when the bandwidth utilization on a router exceeds 90%. Event-based alarms are triggered by specific network events, such as link up/down events, interface status changes, or protocol errors.

Administrators can configure event-based alarms using RMON management stations, specifying the event type, severity level, and action to be taken when the event occurs. For example, administrators can configure an alarm to alert them via SMS or syslog when a critical interface goes down. Combination alarms combine threshold-based and event-based criteria, allowing administrators to configure complex alarms based on multiple conditions. Administrators can configure combination alarms using RMON management stations, specifying the combination of threshold values and event types that trigger the alarm, as well as the action to be taken when the alarm is triggered. For example, administrators can configure an alarm to alert them via SNMP trap when the CPU utilization on a router exceeds 90% for more than 5 minutes, and a link goes down on a critical interface. RMON alarm and event management enable administrators to monitor network devices and services continuously and detect potential issues before they impact network performance or availability. By configuring alarms and events based on specific criteria, administrators can receive timely alerts and notifications, allowing them to take proactive measures to address network issues and minimize their impact on network operations. RMON management stations provide a user-friendly interface for configuring and managing alarms and events, allowing administrators to define alarm thresholds, event types, and actions easily. Administrators can use RMON management stations to view the status of alarms and events, acknowledge alarms, and configure notification settings, such as email recipients, SNMP trap receivers, or syslog servers. RMON alarm and event management can be deployed in various network environments, including enterprise networks, service provider networks, and data center networks. Administrators can deploy RMON probes on network devices, such as routers, switches, and firewalls, to capture network traffic and monitor device status and performance. RMON management stations can be deployed on dedicated servers or virtual machines, providing centralized management and monitoring of RMON probes across the network. By deploying RMON alarm and event management, administrators can improve the reliability and availability of network services, reduce downtime and service disruptions, and enhance the overall efficiency of network operations. In summary, RMON Alarm and Event Management are essential tools for network administrators, providing them with the ability to monitor network devices and services continuously and detect potential issues proactively. By configuring alarms and events based on specific criteria, administrators can receive timely alerts and notifications, allowing them to take proactive measures to address network issues and ensure the reliability and availability of network services.

Chapter 5: Implementing Quality of Service (QoS) Protocols

QoS (Quality of Service) Mechanisms and Techniques are essential components of network management, providing administrators with the means to prioritize and control traffic flows, ensuring optimal performance for critical applications and services. QoS mechanisms and techniques enable administrators to allocate network resources effectively, manage congestion, and guarantee the delivery of high-priority traffic, such as voice, video, and real-time data. One of the key QoS mechanisms is traffic classification, which involves identifying and categorizing traffic flows based on specific criteria, such as source/destination IP addresses, port numbers, or protocol types. Traffic classification allows administrators to differentiate between different types of traffic and apply QoS policies accordingly. Administrators can use CLI commands such as 'class-map' on Cisco devices to define traffic classes based on matching criteria, specifying the match criteria and assigning them to specific classes. Once traffic classes are defined, administrators can apply QoS policies to prioritize and manage traffic flows using QoS techniques such as traffic policing, shaping, and queuing. Traffic policing is a QoS technique used to control the rate of traffic flows, ensuring that they comply with predefined traffic contracts or service level agreements (SLAs). Administrators can configure traffic policing using CLI commands such as 'police' on Cisco devices, specifying the traffic rate, burst size, and action to be taken when traffic exceeds the specified rate. Traffic shaping is another QoS technique used to control the rate of traffic flows, smoothing out bursts of traffic to ensure that they conform to predefined traffic profiles. Administrators can configure traffic shaping using CLI commands such as 'shape' on Cisco devices, specifying the desired traffic rate, burst size, and shaping parameters. Traffic shaping helps to prevent network congestion and improve the overall performance of critical applications and services. Queuing is a QoS technique used to prioritize traffic flows and manage congestion in network queues. Administrators can configure queuing using CLI commands such as 'priority' and 'bandwidth' on Cisco devices, specifying the queuing method, priority levels, and bandwidth allocations for different traffic classes. Queuing allows administrators to give preferential treatment to high-priority traffic, such as voice and video, ensuring that it receives adequate bandwidth and low latency. Another QoS technique is traffic marking, which involves setting QoS markings in packet headers to classify traffic and prioritize it accordingly. Administrators can use CLI commands such as 'set dscp' on Cisco devices to mark packets with Differentiated Services Code Point (DSCP) values, specifying the desired QoS markings and priorities for different types of traffic. Traffic marking enables downstream devices, such as routers and switches, to prioritize traffic based on QoS markings, ensuring that high-priority traffic receives preferential treatment throughout the network. Traffic shaping helps to prevent network congestion and improve the overall performance of critical applications and services. Administrators can deploy QoS mechanisms and techniques in various network environments, including enterprise networks, service provider networks, and data center networks, to optimize network performance and ensure the reliable delivery of critical applications and services. By implementing QoS policies and techniques, administrators can prioritize traffic flows, manage congestion, and meet the performance requirements of diverse applications and users. QoS mechanisms and techniques play a crucial role in enabling organizations to deliver high-quality services and maintain a competitive edge in today's fast-paced digital world. In summary, QoS Mechanisms and Techniques are essential tools for network administrators, providing them with the means to prioritize and control traffic flows, ensuring optimal performance for critical applications and services. By deploying QoS mechanisms and techniques, administrators can optimize network resources, manage congestion, and guarantee the delivery of high-priority traffic, enhancing the overall reliability and efficiency of network operations. QoS (Quality of Service) Mechanisms and Techniques are fundamental aspects of network management, serving to optimize the performance and reliability of network traffic by prioritizing critical data flows over less essential ones. These mechanisms and techniques are essential for ensuring that networks can effectively handle the diverse range of traffic types and applications present in modern digital environments. One primary QoS mechanism is traffic classification, which involves identifying and categorizing different types of traffic based on specific attributes such as source/destination IP addresses, port numbers, or protocol types. By classifying traffic, administrators can apply different QoS policies to prioritize critical traffic flows while appropriately managing less important ones. For instance, on Cisco devices, administrators can utilize the 'class-map' command to define traffic classes based on specified criteria, allowing for granular control over traffic prioritization. Once traffic classes are established, administrators can employ various QoS techniques to manage and prioritize traffic accordingly. One such technique is traffic policing, which enables administrators to control the rate of traffic flows to ensure they adhere to predefined traffic contracts or service level agreements (SLAs). Using commands like 'police' on Cisco devices, administrators can set traffic rate limits, burst sizes, and actions to take when traffic exceeds specified thresholds, effectively managing bandwidth usage and preventing congestion. Another critical QoS technique is traffic shaping, which smooths out bursts of traffic to conform to predetermined traffic profiles, thereby preventing network congestion and ensuring more consistent performance for critical applications. Administrators can configure traffic shaping using commands such as 'shape' on Cisco devices, specifying desired traffic rates, burst sizes, and shaping parameters to align traffic flows with available network resources. Queuing is also a vital QoS technique, allowing administrators to prioritize traffic flows in network queues to manage congestion effectively. Using commands like 'priority' and 'bandwidth' on Cisco devices, administrators can specify queuing methods, priority levels, and bandwidth allocations for different traffic classes, ensuring that high-priority traffic receives preferential treatment and minimizing delays for critical applications. Additionally, traffic marking plays a crucial role in QoS by setting QoS markings in packet headers to classify and prioritize traffic throughout the network. Commands like 'set dscp' on Cisco devices can be used to mark packets with Differentiated Services Code Point (DSCP) values, enabling downstream devices to prioritize traffic based on QoS markings and ensure consistent performance across the network. Deploying QoS mechanisms and techniques requires careful planning and configuration to align with the specific needs and priorities of the network environment. Administrators must consider factors such as traffic patterns, application requirements, and available network resources when designing and implementing QoS policies. Furthermore, regular monitoring and adjustment of QoS configurations are essential to adapt to changing network conditions and ensure optimal performance over time. Overall, QoS mechanisms and techniques are indispensable tools for network administrators, enabling them to manage and prioritize traffic effectively to meet the performance and reliability requirements of modern digital networks. By leveraging QoS capabilities, administrators can optimize network resources, enhance user experience, and ensure the consistent delivery of critical applications and services.

Chapter 6: Managing Bandwidth with Traffic Control Protocols

Traffic Control Fundamentals are essential aspects of network management, encompassing a range of techniques and strategies to regulate the flow of data across networks, ensuring optimal performance and resource utilization. One fundamental aspect of traffic control is traffic shaping, which involves controlling the rate of data transmission to match available bandwidth and prevent congestion. Administrators can utilize commands such as 'tc' on Linux systems to implement traffic shaping policies, specifying parameters such as bandwidth limits, burst sizes, and shaping algorithms to regulate traffic flow effectively. By shaping traffic, administrators can smooth out bursts of data and ensure that critical applications receive sufficient bandwidth to operate efficiently. Another critical aspect of traffic control is traffic policing, which involves monitoring and enforcing traffic rate limits to prevent network congestion and maintain quality of service. Using commands like 'police' on Cisco devices, administrators can set traffic rate limits, burst sizes, and actions to take when traffic exceeds predefined thresholds, allowing for proactive management of network resources and bandwidth allocation. Additionally, traffic classification plays a vital role in traffic control by categorizing data flows based on specific attributes such as source/destination IP addresses, port numbers, or protocol types. Administrators can use commands like 'class-map' on Cisco devices to define traffic classes and apply different traffic control policies based on the classification criteria, allowing for granular control over traffic prioritization and resource allocation. Queuing is another essential traffic control mechanism that involves managing the order in which packets are transmitted from network queues, allowing administrators to prioritize critical traffic and ensure timely delivery. Commands such as 'priority' and 'bandwidth' on Cisco devices can be used to configure queuing parameters, specifying priority levels and bandwidth allocations for different traffic classes to optimize network performance and reduce latency. Additionally, packet scheduling algorithms such as Weighted Fair Queuing (WFQ) and Class-Based Weighted Fair Queuing (CBWFQ) can be deployed to allocate bandwidth dynamically based on traffic characteristics and priority levels. Network administrators can also employ access control lists (ACLs) to control traffic flow based on specific criteria such as source/destination IP addresses, port numbers, or protocol types. By configuring

ACLs using commands like 'access-list' on Cisco devices, administrators can filter traffic and enforce security policies to protect network resources and mitigate potential threats. Furthermore, Quality of Service (QoS) mechanisms such as Differentiated Services (DiffServ) and Integrated Services (IntServ) can be implemented to prioritize traffic and ensure consistent performance for critical applications. By configuring QoS policies using commands like 'qos' on Cisco devices, administrators can classify, prioritize, and manage traffic based on service requirements and business priorities, enabling efficient resource utilization and enhancing user experience. Deploying traffic control mechanisms requires careful planning and configuration to align with the specific requirements and objectives of the network environment. Administrators must consider factors such as traffic patterns, application requirements, and available network resources when designing and implementing traffic control policies. Regular monitoring and analysis of network traffic are also essential to identify potential bottlenecks and performance issues, allowing administrators to adjust traffic control policies accordingly and optimize network performance over time. In summary, Traffic Control Fundamentals are essential for managing and regulating the flow of data across networks, ensuring optimal performance, and resource utilization. By implementing traffic shaping, policing, classification, queuing, and other traffic control mechanisms, administrators can effectively manage network traffic, prioritize critical applications, and maintain quality of service to meet the demands of modern digital environments. Traffic shaping and policing strategies are essential components of network management, allowing administrators to regulate the flow of data and optimize network performance. One commonly used technique is traffic shaping, which involves controlling the rate of data transmission to match available bandwidth and prevent congestion. Administrators can implement traffic shaping using commands such as 'tc' on Linux systems or 'shape' on Cisco devices, specifying parameters such as bandwidth limits, burst sizes, and shaping algorithms to smooth out bursts of data and ensure consistent performance for critical applications. By shaping traffic, administrators can prioritize important data flows and prevent less critical traffic from overwhelming network resources. Another important strategy is traffic policing, which involves monitoring and enforcing traffic rate limits to prevent network congestion and maintain quality of service. Using commands like 'police' on Cisco devices, administrators can set traffic rate limits, burst sizes, and actions to take when traffic exceeds predefined thresholds, allowing for proactive management of network resources and bandwidth allocation. Traffic policing helps to ensure fair access to network resources and prevent individual users or applications from monopolizing bandwidth, thereby improving overall network performance and reliability. Additionally, administrators can deploy traffic classification techniques to categorize data flows based on specific attributes such as source/destination IP addresses, port numbers, or protocol types. By classifying traffic, administrators can apply different traffic shaping and policing policies based on the classification criteria, allowing for granular control over traffic prioritization and resource allocation. Commands such as 'class-map' on Cisco devices can be used to define traffic classes and apply specific policies to each class, enabling administrators to optimize network performance and ensure consistent delivery of critical applications. Queuing is another important strategy for managing traffic and preventing congestion in network queues. By configuring queuing parameters using commands like 'priority' and 'bandwidth' on Cisco devices, administrators can prioritize traffic flows and allocate bandwidth based on predefined criteria, ensuring that critical applications receive preferential treatment and minimizing delays for end users. Additionally, administrators can deploy packet scheduling algorithms such as Weighted Fair Queuing (WFQ) or

Class-Based Weighted Fair Queuing (CBWFQ) to allocate bandwidth dynamically based on traffic characteristics and priority levels. These algorithms help to optimize network resources and ensure fair access to bandwidth for all users and applications. Access control lists (ACLs) can also be used to control traffic flow and enforce security policies based on specific criteria such as source/destination IP addresses, port numbers, or protocol types. By configuring ACLs using commands like 'access-list' on Cisco devices, administrators can filter traffic and restrict access to network resources, thereby improving network security and mitigating potential threats. Furthermore, Quality of Service (QoS) mechanisms such as Differentiated Services (DiffServ) or Integrated Services (IntServ) can be implemented to prioritize traffic and ensure consistent performance for critical applications. By configuring QoS policies using commands like 'qos' on Cisco devices, administrators can classify, prioritize, and manage traffic based on service requirements and business priorities, enabling efficient resource utilization and enhancing user experience. Deploying traffic shaping and policing strategies requires careful planning and configuration to align with the specific needs and objectives of the network environment. Administrators must consider factors such as traffic patterns, application requirements, and available network resources when designing and implementing traffic management policies. Regular monitoring and analysis of network traffic are also essential to identify potential bottlenecks and performance issues, allowing administrators to adjust traffic management policies accordingly and optimize network performance over time. In summary, Traffic Shaping and Policing Strategies are essential for managing and optimizing network traffic, ensuring optimal performance, and resource utilization. By implementing these strategies, administrators can effectively prioritize critical applications, prevent network congestion, and maintain quality of service to meet the demands of modern digital environments.

Chapter 7: Network Monitoring and Analysis with Packet Sniffing Protocols

Packet sniffing fundamentals are crucial aspects of network analysis and troubleshooting, providing administrators with insights into network traffic and helping them diagnose issues and optimize performance. One of the most common tools used for packet sniffing is Wireshark, a powerful open-source packet analyzer that allows administrators to capture, view, and analyze network packets in real-time. Using Wireshark, administrators can gain detailed visibility into the contents of individual packets, including source/destination IP addresses, port numbers, protocol types, and payload data. To capture packets using Wireshark, administrators can simply select the desired network interface and start a capture session, allowing them to monitor traffic in real-time or save captured packets for later analysis. In addition to Wireshark, other command-line packet sniffing tools such as tcpdump or tshark can be used to capture packets directly from the command line. For example, administrators can use the 'tcpdump' command on Linux systems to capture packets on a specific network interface and save them to a file for later analysis. Packet sniffing can be used for various purposes, including network troubleshooting, performance monitoring, security analysis, and protocol debugging. Administrators can use packet sniffing tools to identify network errors, diagnose connectivity issues, and troubleshoot performance problems by analyzing packet headers, identifying patterns, and pinpointing the root cause of issues. Moreover, packet sniffing can be invaluable for monitoring network performance and identifying potential bottlenecks or areas of congestion. By capturing and analyzing network traffic, administrators can gain insights into traffic patterns, application behavior, and bandwidth usage, allowing them to optimize network resources and improve overall performance. Packet sniffing also plays a crucial role in network security, allowing administrators to detect and analyze suspicious or malicious activity on the network. By monitoring packet headers and payload data, administrators can identify security threats such as unauthorized access attempts, malware infections, and data breaches, enabling them to take proactive measures to protect the network and mitigate potential risks. Additionally, packet sniffing can be used for protocol analysis and debugging, allowing administrators to analyze the behavior of network protocols and identify protocol-related issues. By examining packet headers and payload data, administrators can identify protocol violations, misconfigurations, or compatibility issues, enabling them to troubleshoot and resolve protocol-related problems effectively. However, it's essential to note that packet sniffing raises privacy and security concerns, as it can capture sensitive information such as usernames, passwords, and confidential data transmitted over the network. Administrators must ensure that packet sniffing is conducted in compliance with applicable laws, regulations, and organizational policies, and take appropriate measures to protect the privacy and security of network data. Moreover, packet sniffing should only be performed on networks and systems that administrators have explicit authorization to access, and sensitive information should be encrypted or masked to prevent unauthorized access or disclosure. In summary, packet sniffing fundamentals are essential for network analysis, troubleshooting, and security, providing administrators with valuable insights into network traffic and helping them diagnose and resolve issues effectively. By using packet sniffing tools such as Wireshark, tcpdump, or tshark, administrators can capture, analyze, and interpret network packets to gain visibility into network behavior, optimize performance, and enhance security. However, it's crucial to conduct packet sniffing responsibly and ethically, ensuring compliance with privacy and security regulations and protecting the confidentiality and integrity of

network   data.
Packet analysis tools and methods are indispensable components of network management, enabling administrators to capture, inspect, and interpret network packets to gain insights into network behavior and diagnose issues effectively. One of the most widely used packet analysis tools is Wireshark, a powerful open-source packet analyzer that provides a comprehensive suite of features for capturing, dissecting, and analyzing network traffic. Administrators can deploy Wireshark by simply launching the application and selecting the network interface to capture packets from. Once packets are captured, Wireshark provides a user-friendly interface for viewing packet details, including source/destination IP addresses, port numbers, protocol types, and packet payloads. Moreover, Wireshark offers advanced filtering and search capabilities, allowing administrators to focus on specific packets or protocols of interest and quickly identify relevant information. Another popular packet analysis tool is tcpdump, a command-line packet sniffer available on Unix-like operating systems. Administrators can use tcpdump to capture packets directly from the command line, specifying parameters such as the network interface to capture packets from and optional filtering criteria to narrow down the captured traffic. For example, the command 'tcpdump -i eth0' captures

packets from the eth0 interface, while 'tcpdump port 80' captures packets with destination port 80. Tcpdump provides a wealth of options for filtering and displaying captured packets, making it a versatile tool for network troubleshooting and analysis. Additionally, tshark, the command-line counterpart to Wireshark, offers similar functionality for capturing and analyzing packets from the command line. Administrators can use tshark to perform packet captures and apply display filters, statistics, and protocol dissectors to analyze captured packets efficiently. Tshark is particularly useful for scripting and automation, allowing administrators to integrate packet analysis tasks into their workflow and perform automated network diagnostics. When performing packet analysis, administrators can employ various methods and techniques to extract valuable information from captured packets. One common method is protocol analysis, which involves dissecting and analyzing individual protocol headers to understand how different network protocols operate and interact. Administrators can use Wireshark's built-in protocol dissectors to inspect protocol headers and decode packet contents, enabling them to identify protocol-specific issues and anomalies. Moreover, statistical analysis techniques such as traffic profiling and flow analysis can provide insights into traffic patterns, bandwidth usage, and network performance. Administrators can use Wireshark's statistics features to generate traffic summaries, protocol distribution charts, and conversation statistics, allowing them to visualize and analyze network traffic patterns effectively. Furthermore, behavioral analysis techniques such as anomaly detection and pattern recognition can help administrators identify abnormal or suspicious network behavior indicative of security threats or performance issues. By comparing observed network behavior to baseline norms and predefined thresholds, administrators can detect anomalies such as sudden spikes in traffic, unusual protocol usage, or unauthorized access attempts. Packet analysis tools also support forensic analysis, allowing administrators to reconstruct network events and investigate security incidents or network breaches. Administrators can use packet capture files as evidence in forensic investigations, analyzing packet contents and timestamps to reconstruct the sequence of events leading up to a security incident. Moreover, packet analysis tools such as Wireshark provide features for exporting packet capture data in various formats, enabling administrators to share captured packets with forensic analysts or law enforcement agencies for further analysis. In summary, packet analysis tools and methods are essential for network troubleshooting, performance monitoring, and security analysis, providing administrators with the means to capture, inspect, and interpret network packets effectively. By deploying tools such as Wireshark, tcpdump, or tshark, and employing methods such as protocol analysis, statistical analysis, behavioral analysis, and forensic analysis, administrators can gain valuable insights into network behavior, diagnose issues, and respond to security incidents promptly. However, it's essential to use packet analysis tools responsibly and ethically, ensuring compliance with privacy and security regulations and protecting the confidentiality and integrity of network data.

Chapter 8: Automating Tasks with Scripting and Protocol Integration

Scripting languages for network automation play a pivotal role in streamlining network management tasks, enabling administrators to automate repetitive processes, deploy configurations, and orchestrate network operations efficiently. Python, in particular, has emerged as a dominant language for network automation due to its simplicity, readability, and extensive library support. Administrators can utilize Python scripts to interact with network devices, retrieve device configurations, parse data, and execute configuration changes programmatically. By leveraging Python's built-in libraries such as Paramiko and Netmiko, administrators can establish SSH connections to network devices and execute commands remotely, facilitating tasks such as backup, configuration deployment, and firmware upgrades. Additionally, Python's rich ecosystem of third-party libraries, including NAPALM and pyATS, provides advanced capabilities for network automation, such as device abstraction, validation, and testing. With NAPALM, administrators can abstract device configurations into a unified data model, enabling consistent management across different vendor platforms and simplifying automation workflows. Similarly, pyATS offers a comprehensive framework for network testing and validation, allowing administrators to automate testing scenarios, verify network configurations, and ensure compliance with network policies. Another scripting language commonly used for network automation is Bash, a shell scripting language available on Unix-like operating systems. Bash scripts are particularly useful for automating routine administrative tasks, such as file management, log rotation, and system monitoring. Administrators can use Bash scripts to execute commands sequentially, perform conditional logic, and iterate over lists of devices or files. For example, administrators can write Bash scripts to automate device configuration backups by connecting to multiple devices via SSH and executing backup commands in a loop. Bash scripts can also be used to parse and manipulate text-based configuration files, extract relevant information, and generate reports or alerts based on predefined criteria. Moreover, administrators can leverage Bash's integration with system utilities and command-line tools to orchestrate complex automation workflows and integrate network management tasks with other system processes. While Python and Bash are widely used for network automation, other scripting languages such as Perl and Ruby also offer capabilities for automating network tasks. Perl, known for its powerful text processing features, is well-suited for tasks involving regex pattern matching, file parsing, and data manipulation. Administrators can use Perl scripts to automate tasks such as log analysis, data extraction, and report generation, leveraging Perl's extensive library support and community-contributed modules. Similarly, Ruby, with its elegant syntax and robust object-oriented features, provides a versatile platform for network automation. Administrators can use Ruby scripts to build automation frameworks, develop custom tools, and integrate with APIs for device management and configuration. Ruby's active community and ecosystem of gems offer libraries and frameworks for network automation, making it a viable option for building scalable and maintainable automation solutions. In addition to scripting languages, configuration management tools such as Ansible, Puppet, and Chef are widely used for automating network infrastructure. These tools leverage declarative configuration files or playbooks to define desired states and automatically enforce configurations across network devices. Administrators can use Ansible playbooks, written in YAML syntax, to describe configuration tasks, manage inventory, and execute tasks across multiple devices simultaneously. With Puppet and

Chef, administrators can define configuration policies using domain-specific languages (DSLs) and enforce configurations consistently across heterogeneous environments. These configuration management tools offer capabilities for idempotent configuration deployment, change tracking, and infrastructure as code (IaC), enabling administrators to automate network provisioning, configuration drift remediation, and compliance enforcement. In summary, scripting languages play a crucial role in network automation, enabling administrators to automate routine tasks, streamline operations, and improve efficiency in network management. Whether using Python, Bash, Perl, Ruby, or configuration management tools like Ansible, Puppet, and Chef, administrators have a range of options for automating network infrastructure and enhancing agility in network operations. By leveraging scripting languages and automation frameworks, administrators can reduce manual effort, minimize errors, and accelerate the pace of innovation in network management and configuration.

Protocol integration for automated workflows is a fundamental aspect of modern network management, allowing administrators to orchestrate complex tasks and streamline operations by integrating disparate protocols and systems seamlessly. One common approach to protocol integration is through the use of application programming interfaces (APIs), which enable different systems and applications to communicate and exchange data programmatically. APIs provide standardized interfaces for accessing and manipulating data, allowing administrators to automate workflows by leveraging the capabilities of various systems and services. For example, network devices often expose APIs that allow administrators to retrieve device configurations, modify settings, and monitor performance metrics remotely. By interacting with device APIs, administrators can automate tasks such as configuration backup, compliance checks, and provisioning, reducing manual effort and ensuring consistency across the network. Additionally, administrators can integrate network devices with external systems and applications using APIs, enabling cross-platform automation and enhancing the functionality of network infrastructure. Another approach to protocol integration is through the use of messaging protocols such as Simple Network Management Protocol (SNMP) or Syslog, which facilitate communication and event notification between network devices and management systems. SNMP, for instance, enables administrators to monitor and manage network devices by querying device agents for status information and receiving traps or notifications when predefined events occur. By configuring SNMP agents on network devices and setting up a central SNMP management system, administrators can collect device metrics, detect faults, and automate response actions based on predefined thresholds or conditions. Similarly, Syslog allows network devices to send log messages to a centralized logging server, enabling administrators to analyze and correlate log data from multiple sources. By parsing and analyzing Syslog messages, administrators can detect security incidents, troubleshoot network issues, and automate incident response workflows. Moreover, administrators can leverage event-driven automation frameworks such as Event-Driven Automation (EDA) or Event-Driven Architecture (EDA) to orchestrate workflows based on real-time events and triggers. These frameworks enable administrators to define event-driven rules and actions that automatically execute in response to specific events or conditions. For example, administrators can configure event-driven rules to trigger configuration changes, route updates, or service deployments based on network events such as link failures, traffic spikes, or security alerts. By harnessing the power of event-driven automation, administrators can proactively respond to dynamic network conditions, minimize downtime, and optimize performance. In addition to APIs, messaging protocols, and event-driven automation, administrators can integrate network protocols using middleware platforms or integration tools that provide abstraction layers and adapters for interoperability. These platforms enable administrators to connect and synchronize data between different systems, applications, and protocols, facilitating seamless communication and data exchange. For instance, integration platforms such as Apache Camel or MuleSoft offer support for a wide range of protocols and data formats, allowing administrators to build integration flows that transform and route data between disparate systems with ease. By configuring integration flows and mappings, administrators can automate data synchronization, workflow orchestration, and business process automation across heterogeneous environments. Furthermore, administrators can leverage scripting languages such as Python, Ruby, or JavaScript to develop custom integration scripts or plugins that bridge the gap between different protocols and systems. These scripts can interact with APIs, parse data formats, and perform protocol conversions, enabling administrators to build custom integration solutions tailored to their specific requirements. For example, administrators can use Python scripts to fetch data from a RESTful API, transform it into a format compatible with SNMP, and send it to a network monitoring system for further analysis. By combining scripting languages with APIs and messaging protocols, administrators can create powerful integration solutions that automate workflows, enhance visibility, and improve operational efficiency in network management. In summary, protocol integration is essential for automating workflows and streamlining operations in modern network management. By leveraging APIs, messaging protocols, event-driven automation, middleware platforms, and scripting languages, administrators can integrate disparate systems, applications, and protocols to orchestrate complex tasks and optimize performance in network infrastructure. Whether automating configuration management, monitoring and alerting, or incident response, effective protocol integration enables administrators to automate routine tasks, improve agility, and adapt to evolving network requirements.

Chapter 9: Centralized Management with Network Management Systems (NMS)

Network Management Systems (NMS) form the backbone of modern network infrastructure, providing essential capabilities for monitoring, configuring, and optimizing network performance. NMS architecture encompasses a range of components and features designed to facilitate efficient network management and ensure the reliability and security of network operations. At the core of NMS architecture is the management server, which serves as the central hub for monitoring and controlling network devices. The management server hosts the NMS application and database, storing configuration data, performance metrics, and event logs related to network devices and services. Administrators can interact with the management server through a web-based user interface or command-line interface (CLI), accessing features such as device discovery, inventory management, and performance monitoring. To deploy an NMS, administrators can use software packages such as Nagios, Zabbix, or SolarWinds, which provide pre-configured solutions for monitoring and managing network infrastructure. For example, to install Nagios, administrators can use package managers such as apt or yum to download and install the Nagios Core package on a Linux server. Once installed, administrators can configure Nagios by editing configuration files in the /etc/nagios directory, specifying parameters such as host groups, service checks, and notification settings. Similarly, administrators can deploy Zabbix by downloading the Zabbix server and agent packages from the official website and installing them on separate servers. After installation, administrators can access the Zabbix web interface to configure hosts, define monitoring templates, and set up alerting and reporting features. In addition to the management server, NMS architecture includes agent software installed on network devices to facilitate communication and data collection. Agents run on network devices such as routers, switches, and servers, collecting device metrics, status information, and event logs and forwarding them to the management server for analysis and processing. Administrators can deploy agents using configuration management tools such as Ansible or Puppet, which automate the installation and configuration of agent software across multiple devices. For example, to deploy the SNMP agent on a Cisco router using Ansible, administrators can create a playbook that specifies the desired SNMP configuration settings and uses the ios_config module to apply the configuration to the router. Similarly, administrators can use Puppet manifests to define the desired SNMP configuration and apply it to devices in the network. Once deployed, agents communicate with the management server using standardized protocols such as Simple Network Management Protocol (SNMP), Syslog, or Windows Management Instrumentation (WMI), depending on the device type and vendor. SNMP is a widely used protocol for monitoring and managing network devices, allowing administrators to query device metrics, receive traps or notifications, and perform configuration changes remotely. To enable SNMP on a device, administrators can use CLI commands such as snmp-server community and snmp-server host to configure SNMP community strings and trap destinations, respectively. Once SNMP is enabled, the device can communicate with the management server, providing real-time status updates and performance metrics. Syslog is another essential protocol for NMS architecture, allowing network devices to send log messages to a centralized logging server for analysis and troubleshooting. Administrators can configure syslog on network devices using CLI commands such as logging host and logging facility to specify the syslog server address and message severity level, respectively. By centralizing log messages from multiple devices, administrators can identify security incidents, track system events, and diagnose network issues effectively. Moreover, NMS architecture includes features such as fault management, performance monitoring, configuration management, and security management to address various aspects of network management. Fault management features enable administrators to detect, isolate, and resolve network faults proactively, minimizing downtime and ensuring service availability. Performance monitoring features provide insights into network performance and utilization, allowing administrators to identify bottlenecks, optimize resource allocation, and plan capacity upgrades. Configuration management features enable administrators to automate device provisioning, configuration backups, and compliance checks, ensuring consistency and adherence to network policies. Security management features enable administrators to enforce access controls, monitor user activity, and detect security threats, safeguarding the integrity and confidentiality of network data. In summary, NMS architecture encompasses a range of components and features designed to facilitate efficient network management and ensure the reliability and security of network operations. By deploying an NMS, administrators can monitor, configure, and optimize network infrastructure, improving performance, reducing downtime, and enhancing the overall reliability of the network. Whether using open-source solutions or commercial offerings, NMS architecture provides a flexible and scalable framework for managing network infrastructure and adapting to evolving business requirements.

NMS deployment and configuration are critical steps in establishing an effective network management infrastructure, enabling administrators to monitor, control, and optimize network devices and services efficiently. To deploy an NMS, administrators must first select an appropriate software solution that aligns with their organization's requirements and infrastructure. Popular NMS options include open-source platforms like Nagios, Zabbix, and Cacti, as well as commercial offerings such as SolarWinds, PRTG Network Monitor, and ManageEngine OpManager. Once a suitable NMS solution is chosen, administrators can begin the deployment process by installing the NMS software on a dedicated server or virtual machine. For instance, to deploy Nagios Core, administrators can download the Nagios Core tarball from the official website and extract it to a directory on the server using the tar command. Next, administrators can run the ./configure, make, and make install commands to compile and install Nagios Core from source. After installation, administrators can configure Nagios by editing the main configuration file (nagios.cfg) and defining parameters such as contact information, notification settings, and host groups. Similarly, administrators can deploy Zabbix by downloading the Zabbix server and agent packages from the official website and installing them on separate servers. Once installed, administrators can access the Zabbix web interface to configure hosts, set up monitoring templates, and define alerting rules. Configuration of NMS involves defining network devices, services, and performance metrics that need to be monitored and managed. Administrators can use the NMS web interface or configuration files to specify devices, services, and thresholds for monitoring. For example, in Nagios, administrators can define hosts and services by creating configuration files in the /etc/nagios/conf.d directory, specifying parameters such as host IP address, service type, and monitoring checks. Similarly, in Zabbix, administrators can add hosts and items through the web interface, specifying parameters such as host name, SNMP community string, and monitoring intervals. Additionally, administrators can configure notification settings in the NMS to receive alerts and notifications when predefined thresholds are exceeded or events occur. Notifications can be configured to be sent via email, SMS, or other communication channels to ensure timely response to network issues. For example, in Nagios, administrators can define contact groups, notification commands, and escalation policies in the contacts.cfg and commands.cfg files. Similarly, in Zabbix, administrators can configure media types, users, and actions through the web interface to enable alerting and notification features. After configuring hosts, services, and notifications, administrators can deploy monitoring agents on network devices to collect performance data and transmit it to the NMS for analysis. Monitoring agents run on network devices such as routers, switches, and servers, collecting device metrics, status information, and event logs and forwarding them to the NMS server for processing. Administrators can deploy monitoring agents using configuration management tools such as Ansible or Puppet, which automate the installation and configuration of agent software across multiple devices. For instance, to deploy the SNMP agent on a Cisco router using Ansible, administrators can create a playbook that specifies the desired SNMP configuration settings and uses the ios_config module to apply the configuration to the router. Similarly, administrators can use Puppet manifests to define the desired SNMP configuration and apply it to devices in the network. Once deployed, monitoring agents communicate with the NMS server using standardized protocols such as Simple Network Management Protocol (SNMP), Syslog, or

Windows Management Instrumentation (WMI), depending on the device type and vendor. SNMP is a widely used protocol for monitoring and managing network devices, allowing administrators to query device metrics, receive traps or notifications, and perform configuration changes remotely. To enable SNMP on a device, administrators can use CLI commands such as snmp-server community and snmp-server host to configure SNMP community strings and trap destinations, respectively. Once SNMP is enabled, the device can communicate with the NMS server, providing real-time status updates and performance metrics. Syslog is another essential protocol for NMS configuration, enabling network devices to send log messages to a centralized logging server for analysis and troubleshooting. Administrators can configure syslog on network devices using CLI commands such as logging host and logging facility to specify the syslog server address and message severity level, respectively. By centralizing log messages from multiple devices, administrators can identify security incidents, track system events, and diagnose network issues effectively. In summary, NMS deployment and configuration are essential processes in establishing an effective network management infrastructure, enabling administrators to monitor, control, and optimize network devices and services efficiently. By selecting an appropriate NMS solution, configuring hosts, services, and notifications, and deploying monitoring agents on network devices, administrators can establish a robust monitoring and management framework to ensure the reliability and security of network operations. Whether using open-source platforms or commercial offerings, effective NMS deployment and configuration are essential for maintaining network performance, minimizing downtime, and ensuring compliance with organizational policies and standards.

Chapter 10: Best Practices and Strategies for Effective Network Management

Network management best practices encompass a range of strategies, techniques, and methodologies aimed at ensuring the reliability, security, and performance of network infrastructure. These practices are essential for optimizing network operations, minimizing downtime, and mitigating security risks. One fundamental best practice is to establish a comprehensive network documentation process, which involves documenting network topology, device configurations, and operational procedures. Proper documentation provides valuable insights into the network environment, facilitating troubleshooting, capacity planning, and compliance audits. Administrators can use tools such as network diagramming software or spreadsheet applications to create and maintain network documentation. For instance, tools like Microsoft Visio or Lucidchart allow administrators to create detailed network diagrams, illustrating the layout of network devices, connections, and configurations. Additionally, administrators can leverage configuration management databases (CMDBs) to store and manage detailed information about network devices, including hardware specifications, software versions, and operational status. Implementing robust network security measures is another critical best practice for network management. Security threats such as malware, unauthorized access, and data breaches pose significant risks to network integrity and confidentiality. To mitigate these risks, administrators should implement a multi-layered security approach, incorporating technologies such as firewalls, intrusion detection systems (IDS), and access control mechanisms. For example, administrators can configure firewalls to filter inbound and outbound traffic based on predefined security policies, using commands such as iptables or firewall-cmd in Linux environments. Additionally, administrators can deploy IDS sensors to monitor network traffic for suspicious activity and generate alerts or notifications when potential threats are detected. Access control mechanisms such as role-based access control (RBAC) or network segmentation can further enhance security by restricting access to sensitive network resources and segregating traffic into separate security zones. Regular security audits and vulnerability assessments are also essential components of network security best practices, enabling administrators to identify and remediate security weaknesses before they can be exploited by attackers. Another critical aspect of network management best practices is proactive monitoring and performance management. Monitoring network performance metrics such as bandwidth utilization, packet loss, and latency provides valuable insights into network health and performance trends. Administrators can use monitoring tools such as SNMP-based network monitoring software or packet sniffers to collect and analyze performance data in real-time. For instance, administrators can use the snmpwalk command to query SNMP-enabled devices and retrieve performance data such as CPU usage, memory utilization, and interface statistics. Packet sniffers such as Wireshark or tcpdump can capture and analyze network traffic, allowing administrators to troubleshoot performance issues, identify bottlenecks, and optimize network configuration settings. Additionally, administrators can implement performance monitoring dashboards or reporting tools to visualize performance data and track key performance indicators (KPIs) over time. These tools enable administrators to identify performance trends, predict potential issues, and take proactive measures to optimize network performance and resource utilization. Configuration management is another critical best practice for network management, ensuring consistency and compliance across network devices and configurations. Administrators should establish standardized configuration templates and deployment procedures to streamline device provisioning and configuration management processes. Configuration management tools such as Ansible, Puppet, or Chef can automate configuration tasks and enforce configuration policies across heterogeneous network environments. For example, administrators can use Ansible playbooks to deploy configuration changes or updates to multiple network devices simultaneously, ensuring consistency and reducing the risk of configuration errors. Regular backups of device configurations are also essential to safeguard against configuration drift, hardware failures, or malicious attacks. Administrators can use commands such as copy running-config startup-config or archive config in Cisco IOS devices to save and archive device configurations periodically. Additionally, administrators can leverage version control systems such as Git or SVN to track changes to configuration files and revert to previous configurations if necessary. Lastly, effective change management practices are crucial for minimizing disruptions and ensuring the stability of network operations. Administrators should establish formal change control processes to review, approve, and document changes to network configurations, policies, or procedures. Change management processes should include procedures for risk assessment, impact analysis, and rollback planning to mitigate the potential impact of changes on network stability and performance. For example, administrators can use change management tools or ticketing systems to log and track change requests, allowing stakeholders to review and approve changes before implementation. Additionally, administrators can implement change windows or maintenance windows to schedule planned changes during periods of low network activity, minimizing the risk of service disruptions. By following network management best practices such as documentation, security, monitoring, configuration management, and change management, organizations can optimize network performance, enhance security posture, and ensure the reliability of network operations. These practices enable administrators to proactively manage network infrastructure, minimize downtime, and mitigate risks, ultimately supporting the organization's strategic goals and objectives. Strategies for proactive network management are essential for maintaining the stability, performance, and security of network infrastructure in today's dynamic IT environments. These strategies involve proactive monitoring, preventive maintenance, and risk mitigation techniques aimed at identifying and addressing potential issues before they impact network operations. One key aspect of proactive network management is implementing robust monitoring solutions that continuously track the health and performance of network devices, services, and applications. Administrators can leverage network monitoring tools such as Nagios, Zabbix, or PRTG Network Monitor to collect real-time data on network traffic, bandwidth utilization, and device availability. These tools enable administrators to set up alerts and notifications for predefined thresholds, allowing them to respond quickly to potential issues before they escalate. For example, administrators can use the snmpwalk command to query SNMP-enabled devices and retrieve performance data such as CPU usage, memory utilization, and interface statistics. Packet sniffers such as Wireshark or tcpdump can capture and analyze network traffic, allowing administrators to troubleshoot performance issues, identify bottlenecks, and optimize network configuration settings. Additionally, administrators can implement performance monitoring dashboards or reporting tools to visualize performance data and track key performance indicators (KPIs) over time. These tools enable administrators to identify performance trends, predict potential issues, and take proactive measures to optimize network performance and resource utilization. Another proactive strategy is to conduct regular preventive maintenance activities to ensure the reliability and availability of network infrastructure. This includes tasks such as firmware updates, patch management, and hardware inspections to address potential vulnerabilities and mitigate security risks. Administrators can use CLI commands such as copy running-config startup-config or archive config in Cisco IOS devices to save and archive device configurations periodically. Additionally, administrators can leverage version control systems such as Git or SVN to track changes to configuration files and revert to previous configurations if necessary. Regular backups of device configurations are also essential to safeguard against configuration drift, hardware failures, or malicious attacks. Administrators can schedule automated backups using tools such as SolarWinds Network Configuration Manager or RANCID to ensure that critical configuration files are backed up regularly. Additionally, administrators can implement change management processes to review, approve, and document changes to network configurations, policies, or procedures. Change management processes should include procedures for risk assessment, impact analysis, and rollback planning to mitigate the potential impact of changes on network stability and performance. For example, administrators can use change management tools or ticketing systems to log and track change requests, allowing stakeholders to review and approve changes before implementation. Furthermore, organizations can implement proactive security measures to protect against cyber threats and unauthorized access to network resources. This includes strategies such as network segmentation, access control, and intrusion detection/prevention systems (IDS/IPS) to identify and mitigate security threats in real-time. Administrators can configure firewalls to filter inbound and outbound traffic based on predefined security policies, using commands such as iptables or firewall-cmd in Linux environments. Additionally, administrators can deploy IDS sensors to monitor network traffic for suspicious activity and generate alerts or notifications when potential threats are detected. Access control mechanisms such as role-based access control (RBAC) or network segmentation can further enhance security by restricting access to sensitive network resources and segregating traffic into separate security zones. Moreover, organizations can leverage threat intelligence feeds and security information and event management (SIEM) systems to correlate security events and identify emerging threats proactively. By implementing these proactive network management strategies, organizations can minimize downtime, optimize performance, and enhance security posture, ultimately improving the reliability and resilience of their network infrastructure. These strategies enable organizations to stay ahead of potential issues, mitigate risks, and ensure that their networks are well-equipped to support business objectives now and in the future.

BOOK 3
SECURING THE NETWORK
PROTOCOLS, PRACTICES, AND STRATEGIES FOR
SAFEGUARDING DATA

ROB BOTWRIGHT

Chapter 1: Understanding Network Security Fundamentals

Understanding the basics of network security is crucial in safeguarding sensitive information, maintaining the integrity of data, and protecting against cyber threats. Network security encompasses a range of measures and protocols designed to prevent unauthorized access, detect and mitigate threats, and ensure the confidentiality, integrity, and availability of network resources. One fundamental aspect of network security is controlling access to network resources through authentication mechanisms such as passwords, biometrics, or multi-factor authentication. Administrators can configure user authentication settings on network devices using commands such as aaa new-model in Cisco IOS devices to enable authentication, authorization, and accounting (AAA) services. Additionally, administrators can implement role-based access control (RBAC) to define and enforce access permissions based on users' roles and responsibilities within the organization. Encryption is another essential component of network security, ensuring that data transmitted over the network remains confidential and secure from eavesdropping or interception by unauthorized parties. Secure communication protocols such as SSL/TLS encrypt data in transit between client and server devices, preventing attackers from intercepting and reading sensitive information. Administrators can configure SSL/TLS encryption on web servers using commands such as openssl or certbot to generate and install SSL certificates, enabling secure HTTPS connections. Network segmentation is a proactive security measure that divides the network into separate segments or subnets, limiting the scope of potential attacks and containing the spread of malware or malicious activity. Administrators can implement network segmentation using VLANs (virtual LANs) to isolate different departments, teams, or sensitive systems from each other, thereby reducing the attack surface and enhancing overall security posture. Additionally, administrators can deploy firewalls to enforce access control policies between network segments, restricting traffic based on source/destination IP addresses, ports, or protocols. Intrusion detection and prevention systems (IDS/IPS) are critical tools for detecting and mitigating suspicious or malicious activity on the network. IDS sensors monitor network traffic for signs of anomalous behavior or known attack patterns, while IPS devices actively block or quarantine malicious traffic to prevent it from reaching its intended target. Administrators can deploy open-source IDS/IPS solutions such as Snort or Suricata to detect and respond to security threats in real-time, using rulesets to identify and alert on potential attacks. Regular security audits and vulnerability assessments are essential for identifying and remediating security weaknesses in the network infrastructure. Administrators can use scanning tools such as Nessus, OpenVAS, or Nmap to conduct comprehensive vulnerability scans, identifying potential security vulnerabilities, misconfigurations, or outdated software versions that could be exploited by attackers. Additionally, administrators can perform penetration testing to simulate real-world attacks and assess the effectiveness of existing security controls in detecting and mitigating threats. Patch management is another critical aspect of network security, ensuring that network devices and software are up-to-date with the latest security patches and updates. Administrators can use tools such as Microsoft WSUS (Windows Server Update Services) or Red Hat Satellite to automate patch deployment and ensure that critical security patches are applied promptly to all devices on the network. Additionally, administrators can configure devices to automatically check for and install updates using commands such as yum update in Linux environments or Windows Update in Windows environments. Employee education and awareness are essential for maintaining a strong security posture, as human error and negligence can often be exploited by attackers to gain unauthorized access to network resources. Organizations should provide regular training and awareness programs to educate employees about common security threats, phishing scams, and best practices for safeguarding sensitive information. By empowering employees to recognize and report security incidents, organizations can create a culture of security awareness and enhance overall resilience against cyber threats. Finally, incident response planning and preparation are critical for effectively responding to security incidents and minimizing their impact on the organization. Administrators should develop and document incident response procedures, including steps for identifying, containing, investigating, and recovering from security breaches or data breaches. Additionally, organizations should conduct regular tabletop exercises or simulations to test the effectiveness of their incident response plans and ensure that key stakeholders are prepared to respond effectively in the event of a security incident. By implementing these fundamental principles and best practices of network security, organizations can create a robust security framework that protects against a wide range of threats and vulnerabilities. From access control and encryption to intrusion detection and incident response, each component plays a vital role in defending against cyber threats and safeguarding sensitive information in today's interconnected world.

Understanding the threat landscape and conducting comprehensive risk assessments are essential steps in developing effective cybersecurity strategies and mitigating potential risks to an organization's assets, data, and operations. The threat landscape refers to the ever-evolving landscape of cyber threats, including malware, ransomware, phishing attacks, insider threats, and advanced persistent threats (APTs), among others. These threats can originate from various sources, including external attackers, malicious insiders, organized cybercrime groups, and nation-state actors, each with their own motivations and objectives. To assess the threat landscape effectively, organizations must stay informed about emerging threats and vulnerabilities through threat intelligence feeds, security advisories, and industry reports from reputable sources such as CERT (Computer Emergency Response Team) or ISACs (Information Sharing and Analysis Centers). Additionally, organizations can leverage security information and event management (SIEM) solutions to aggregate and analyze security logs and telemetry data from across their network infrastructure, enabling them to detect and respond to potential security incidents in real-time. Risk assessment is a systematic process of identifying, evaluating, and prioritizing potential risks to an organization's assets, taking into account the likelihood of occurrence and the potential impact on business operations. Organizations can conduct risk assessments using various methodologies and frameworks, such as NIST SP 800-30, ISO 27005, or the FAIR (Factor Analysis of Information Risk) model, tailored to their specific industry, regulatory requirements, and risk tolerance. The risk assessment process typically involves several key steps, including asset identification, threat identification, vulnerability assessment, risk analysis, and risk mitigation planning. Administrators can use vulnerability scanning tools such as Nessus or OpenVAS to identify potential vulnerabilities in network devices, applications, and systems, scanning for known security vulnerabilities, misconfigurations, and outdated software versions that could be exploited by attackers. Additionally, organizations can conduct penetration testing to simulate real-world attacks and assess the effectiveness of existing security controls in detecting and mitigating threats. By conducting risk assessments regularly, organizations can prioritize security investments and allocate resources effectively to address the most significant risks to their business operations. One common approach to risk assessment is the use of risk matrices or risk heat maps, which visually represent the likelihood and impact of potential risks based on predefined criteria such as severity, likelihood, and business impact. Administrators can use tools such as Microsoft Excel or specialized risk management software to create risk matrices and facilitate risk assessment workshops with key stakeholders to discuss and prioritize identified risks. Risk mitigation strategies aim to reduce the likelihood and impact of potential risks to an acceptable level, balancing the cost of mitigation measures against the potential impact of a security breach or incident. Organizations can implement various risk mitigation measures, including technical controls, administrative controls, and security awareness training for employees. Technical controls such as firewalls, intrusion detection systems (IDS), and endpoint security solutions help detect and prevent unauthorized access to network resources, while administrative controls such as access control policies, security policies, and procedures define the rules and guidelines for acceptable use of information technology resources. Security awareness training educates employees about common security threats, phishing scams, and best practices for safeguarding sensitive information, empowering them to recognize and report security incidents effectively. By implementing a layered approach to risk mitigation, organizations can establish multiple lines of defense against potential threats, reducing the likelihood of successful attacks and minimizing their impact on business operations. Continuous monitoring and reassessment are essential aspects of effective risk management, as the threat landscape is constantly evolving, and new risks may emerge over time. Organizations should establish processes and procedures for monitoring and reviewing security controls, conducting regular security assessments, and updating risk assessments to reflect changes in the business environment, technology landscape, or threat landscape. By maintaining vigilance and adaptability in the face of evolving threats and risks, organizations can enhance their resilience to cyber attacks and protect their assets, data, and operations from potential harm.

Chapter 2: Authentication and Authorization Protocols

Authentication mechanisms and protocols play a vital role in verifying the identity of users, devices, and services accessing a network or system, ensuring that only authorized entities are granted access to sensitive resources. One of the most common authentication mechanisms is username and password authentication, where users provide a username and password combination to authenticate themselves to a system or service. Administrators can configure username and password authentication on network devices using commands such as username [username] password [password] in Cisco IOS devices, creating local user accounts with associated passwords to control access to device management interfaces. However, username and password authentication alone may not provide sufficient security against modern cyber threats, as passwords can be easily compromised through brute-force attacks, phishing scams, or password reuse. To enhance security, organizations can implement multi-factor authentication (MFA) mechanisms that require users to provide multiple forms of authentication before gaining access to a system or service. MFA typically combines something the user knows (e.g., a password) with something the user has (e.g., a mobile device or hardware token) or something the user is (e.g., biometric data such as fingerprints or facial recognition). Common MFA methods include one-time passwords (OTP) generated by authenticator apps or sent via SMS, hardware tokens that generate OTPs, or biometric authentication using fingerprint or facial recognition scanners. Administrators can enable MFA on authentication servers such as RADIUS (Remote Authentication Dial-In User Service) servers or identity providers like Active Directory using configuration options or third-party authentication solutions. Another authentication mechanism widely used in network environments is certificate-based authentication, where digital certificates issued by a trusted certificate authority (CA) are used to authenticate users, devices, or services. Certificates contain cryptographic keys and identifying information, providing a secure means of verifying the identity of parties involved in a communication exchange. Administrators can deploy certificate-based authentication in various scenarios, such as SSL/TLS client authentication for secure web connections, VPN authentication for remote access, or wireless authentication using EAP-TLS (Extensible Authentication Protocol-Transport Layer Security). To implement certificate-based authentication, administrators need to configure certificate authorities to issue digital certificates to users and devices, deploy certificate revocation lists (CRLs) or online certificate status protocol (OCSP) responders to revoke compromised certificates, and configure network devices to validate client certificates during the authentication process. Biometric authentication is another authentication mechanism that relies on unique biological characteristics such as fingerprints, iris patterns, or facial features to verify the identity of users. Biometric authentication provides a high level of security and convenience, as it eliminates the need for users to remember passwords or carry physical tokens. Organizations can deploy biometric authentication systems using specialized biometric scanners or devices integrated with network access control (NAC) solutions, enabling users to authenticate themselves by scanning their biometric traits. However, biometric authentication may raise privacy concerns, as biometric data is sensitive information that must be securely stored and protected against unauthorized access or misuse. Organizations should implement appropriate security measures, such as encryption and access controls, to safeguard biometric data from unauthorized disclosure or tampering. Additionally, administrators should adhere to legal and regulatory requirements governing the collection, storage, and use of biometric data, such as the General Data Protection Regulation (GDPR) in the European Union or the California Consumer Privacy Act (CCPA) in the United States. In summary, authentication mechanisms and protocols are essential components of network security, providing the foundation for controlling access to sensitive resources and protecting against unauthorized access or malicious activity. By implementing robust authentication mechanisms such as multi-factor authentication, certificate-based authentication, and biometric authentication, organizations can strengthen their security posture and mitigate the risk of unauthorized access or data breaches.

Authorization models and practices are fundamental aspects of cybersecurity, governing the permissions and privileges granted to users, devices, or services to access specific resources or perform certain actions within a network or system. One commonly used authorization model is the discretionary access control (DAC) model, where resource owners have the discretion to grant or revoke access permissions to other users or groups based on their own criteria. In the Unix/Linux operating system, administrators can use the chmod command to modify file permissions, allowing or denying read, write, and execute access to files and directories for specific users, groups, or all users. Another authorization model is the mandatory access control (MAC) model, where access permissions are centrally managed and enforced by a security policy defined by a system administrator or security administrator. MAC systems, such as SELinux (Security-Enhanced Linux) or AppArmor, use security labels or security contexts to classify resources and enforce access controls based on predefined rules and policies. Administrators can use tools like setenforce to enable or disable SELinux enforcement mode or audit2allow to generate custom SELinux policy modules to allow specific operations denied by default policies. Role-based access control (RBAC) is another widely used authorization model that assigns permissions to users based on their roles or responsibilities within an organization. RBAC systems define roles with associated permissions and assign users to roles based on their job functions, simplifying access management and ensuring that users only have access to the resources necessary to perform their duties. In Windows environments, administrators can use the Active Directory Users and Computers console to create security groups representing different roles or job functions and assign permissions to these groups on network resources such as file shares or printers. Attribute-based access control (ABAC) is an advanced authorization model that evaluates access decisions based on attributes associated with users, resources, and environmental conditions. ABAC systems use policies that define rules and conditions for access decisions, taking into account various attributes such as user attributes (e.g., department, job title), resource attributes (e.g., sensitivity level, classification), and environmental attributes (e.g., time of day, network location). Administrators can use specialized ABAC solutions or policy management platforms to define and enforce fine-grained access control policies based on a wide range of attributes, providing flexible and dynamic access control capabilities. In cloud computing environments, identity and access management (IAM) services such as AWS IAM or Azure Active Directory provide centralized control over user access to cloud resources, allowing administrators to define policies that specify who can access specific resources and what actions they can perform. IAM policies use JSON-based syntax to define permissions based on actions, resources, and conditions, enabling granular control over access permissions across cloud services and resources. In summary, authorization models and practices are essential components of cybersecurity, enabling organizations to control access to sensitive resources and protect against unauthorized access or misuse. By implementing appropriate authorization models such as DAC, MAC, RBAC, or

ABAC and leveraging IAM services in cloud environments, organizations can enforce access controls effectively and mitigate the risk of data breaches or security incidents.

Chapter 3: Encryption Protocols for Data Protection

Principles of encryption are foundational concepts in cybersecurity, encompassing techniques and algorithms used to secure sensitive information by converting it into a form that is unreadable without the appropriate decryption key. Encryption plays a crucial role in protecting data confidentiality, integrity, and authenticity, safeguarding it from unauthorized access, interception, or tampering. At its core, encryption relies on mathematical algorithms to transform plaintext data into ciphertext, rendering it unintelligible to anyone without the corresponding decryption key. One of the fundamental principles of encryption is the use of cryptographic keys, which are strings of data used to control the encryption and decryption process. These keys can be symmetric, where the same key is used for both encryption and decryption, or asymmetric, where different keys are used for encryption and decryption. In symmetric encryption, algorithms such as the Advanced Encryption Standard (AES) are widely used to encrypt data using a single secret key, which must be kept confidential to maintain the security of encrypted communications. Administrators can use tools like OpenSSL or GPG (GNU Privacy Guard) to encrypt files or messages using symmetric encryption algorithms, specifying the encryption algorithm and providing the encryption key as parameters. Asymmetric encryption, also known as public-key cryptography, uses a pair of mathematically related keys: a public key for encryption and a private key for decryption. The public key can be freely distributed, allowing anyone to encrypt messages or data for the owner of the corresponding private key, while the private key is kept secret and only known to the key owner for decryption. The RSA (Rivest-Shamir-Adleman) algorithm is one of the most commonly used asymmetric encryption algorithms, providing strong security for digital signatures, secure communication, and key exchange protocols. Administrators can generate RSA key pairs using command-line tools like OpenSSL or cryptographic libraries in programming languages like Python, specifying the key size and other parameters to generate keys suitable for their security requirements. Another essential principle of encryption is the concept of encryption modes, which define how plaintext is processed and transformed into ciphertext. Common encryption modes include Electronic Codebook (ECB), Cipher Block Chaining (CBC), Counter (CTR), and Galois/Counter Mode (GCM), each offering different levels of security and performance characteristics. Administrators should carefully select the encryption mode based on their specific use case and security requirements, considering factors such as data confidentiality, integrity, parallelization, and resistance to cryptographic attacks. In addition to encryption algorithms and modes, key management is a critical aspect of encryption, encompassing the generation, distribution, storage, and rotation of cryptographic keys to ensure their confidentiality and integrity. Key management practices include key generation using secure random number generators, key distribution using secure channels or protocols, key storage in protected environments such as hardware security modules (HSMs) or key management systems, and key rotation to limit the exposure of cryptographic keys over time. Organizations can use dedicated key management solutions like AWS Key Management Service (KMS) or Azure Key Vault to centrally manage cryptographic keys and enforce key lifecycle policies, ensuring compliance with regulatory requirements and industry best practices. Additionally, encryption is often combined with other security measures such as authentication, access control, and data integrity verification to provide comprehensive protection against various cyber threats. By applying encryption principles effectively and integrating encryption technologies into their security architecture, organizations can strengthen their defenses and mitigate the risk of data breaches or unauthorized access to sensitive information. Encryption algorithms and protocols constitute the cornerstone of cybersecurity, providing the means to secure sensitive information and communications in various digital environments. These algorithms and protocols employ sophisticated mathematical techniques to transform plaintext data into ciphertext, rendering it unreadable to unauthorized entities without the corresponding decryption keys. One of the most widely used encryption algorithms is the Advanced Encryption Standard (AES), which is renowned for its robustness, efficiency, and widespread adoption across a multitude of applications and industries. AES operates on fixed block sizes of 128 bits and supports key lengths of 128, 192, and 256 bits, offering a high level of security against brute-force attacks. In practical deployments, AES encryption can be implemented using cryptographic libraries such as OpenSSL, where administrators can specify the desired key length and encryption mode, such as CBC or GCM, to encrypt data securely. Another prominent encryption algorithm is the Rivest-Shamir-Adleman (RSA) algorithm, which is widely used for asymmetric encryption, digital signatures, and key exchange protocols. RSA relies on the mathematical properties of large prime numbers and modular arithmetic to facilitate secure communication between parties by enabling encryption with a public key and decryption with a corresponding private key. Administrators can generate RSA key pairs using commands like openssl genrsa to generate a private key and openssl rsa -pubout to derive the corresponding public key for encryption. Alongside symmetric and asymmetric encryption algorithms, hash functions play a crucial role in encryption protocols by generating fixed-size digests or hashes from variable-length input data. Hash functions such as SHA-256 (Secure Hash Algorithm 256-bit) and SHA-3 are commonly used to verify data integrity, authenticate message integrity, and generate digital signatures. For example, administrators can compute the SHA-256 hash of a file using the sha256sum command in Linux or macOS, providing a checksum that can be compared with the original hash to verify data integrity. Encryption protocols, such as Transport Layer Security (TLS) and its predecessor, Secure Sockets Layer (SSL), facilitate secure communication over network connections by encrypting data transmitted between client and server applications. TLS employs a combination of encryption algorithms, including symmetric encryption for bulk data encryption and asymmetric encryption for key exchange and authentication, to establish secure connections and protect against eavesdropping, tampering, and data interception. To configure TLS encryption for web servers, administrators can use tools like OpenSSL to generate SSL/TLS certificates, which contain cryptographic keys and identity information, and configure web servers such as Apache or Nginx to enable TLS encryption for HTTPS connections. In addition to AES, RSA, and TLS, other encryption algorithms and protocols are tailored for specific use cases and security requirements, such as elliptic curve cryptography (ECC), which offers efficient key generation and smaller key sizes compared to traditional asymmetric algorithms like RSA. Moreover, post-quantum cryptography (PQC) algorithms, such as lattice-based cryptography and hash-based cryptography, are being developed to withstand attacks from quantum computers, which could potentially compromise the security of existing encryption schemes. As the threat landscape evolves and computing capabilities advance, ongoing research and development efforts are essential to innovate and enhance encryption algorithms and protocols to address emerging security challenges and maintain the confidentiality, integrity, and authenticity of digital information and communications.

Chapter 4: Securing Network Devices with Access Control Protocols

Access Control Lists (ACLs) serve as fundamental components of network security, enabling administrators to control traffic flow and restrict access to network resources based on defined criteria. ACLs operate at various network layers, including the network layer (Layer 3) and the transport layer (Layer 4), allowing administrators to enforce security policies and filter traffic at different points in the network topology. In Cisco devices and other networking equipment, ACLs are configured using the appropriate command-line interface (CLI) commands, such as access-list in Cisco IOS, to define specific rules or conditions for permitting or denying traffic. For instance, administrators can create a standard ACL to filter traffic based on source IP addresses or a extended ACL to filter traffic based on source and destination IP addresses, port numbers, and protocols. In a typical deployment scenario, administrators define ACL rules based on the principle of least privilege, where access permissions are granted only to the minimum extent necessary for users or devices to perform their intended functions. This helps reduce the attack surface and mitigate the risk of unauthorized access or malicious activity. ACLs can be applied inbound or outbound on network interfaces, allowing administrators to control traffic entering or leaving a specific interface based on the defined rules. In Cisco routers and switches, ACLs are applied to interfaces using the ip access-group command, specifying the direction (inbound or outbound) and the ACL number or name. Additionally, ACLs can be applied to VLAN interfaces, loopback interfaces, or subinterfaces to enforce security policies within virtual LANs or segmented network environments. ACLs support various match criteria, including source and destination IP addresses, source and destination port numbers, protocols (such as TCP, UDP, ICMP), and IP precedence or differentiated services code point (DSCP) values, enabling granular control over traffic flow and behavior. Administrators can leverage ACLs to implement security measures such as filtering unwanted traffic, preventing denial-of-service (DoS) attacks, enforcing network segmentation, and controlling access to sensitive resources or services. However, it's essential to carefully plan and design ACLs to avoid inadvertently blocking legitimate traffic or creating security loopholes. Regular auditing and testing of ACL configurations are crucial to ensuring their effectiveness and compliance with security policies and regulatory requirements. Furthermore, ACLs should be regularly reviewed and updated to adapt to changes in network infrastructure, applications, and security threats. In addition to traditional ACLs, modern network security solutions often incorporate advanced access control mechanisms, such as next-generation firewalls (NGFWs), intrusion prevention systems (IPS), and identity-based access control, to provide enhanced threat detection, contextual awareness, and dynamic policy enforcement capabilities. By combining ACLs with these advanced security technologies, organizations can establish a comprehensive defense-in-depth strategy to protect their networks against a wide range of cyber threats and vulnerabilities.

Role-Based Access Control (RBAC) is a sophisticated access control model widely employed in information security management, providing granular control over resource access based on the roles and responsibilities of users within an organization. RBAC simplifies access management by defining access permissions in terms of roles rather than individual users, streamlining the administration of access controls and minimizing the risk of errors or inconsistencies. In RBAC, access permissions are associated with roles, which are predefined sets of privileges corresponding to specific job functions or organizational roles. These roles encompass a range of permissions required to perform various tasks or operations within the system, such as read, write, execute, or delete access to specific resources or functionalities. To implement RBAC, administrators first define a set of roles that reflect the organization's structure, business processes, and security requirements. This involves identifying distinct job functions, responsibilities, and access requirements across different departments or user groups. Once the roles are defined, administrators assign users to appropriate roles based on their job responsibilities, expertise, and authorization needs. This assignment process is typically facilitated through role assignment mechanisms provided by identity and access management (IAM) systems or directory services, allowing administrators to assign or revoke roles dynamically as users' roles or responsibilities change. The RBAC model also includes the concept of permissions, which define the specific actions or operations that users assigned to a particular role can perform on resources. Permissions are associated with roles, and each role is assigned a set of permissions relevant to its associated job function or level of authority. For example, a network administrator role may have permissions to configure network devices, while a help desk role may only have permissions to reset user passwords. Administrators can define permissions at a fine-grained level, specifying access controls for individual resources, directories, files, or application functionalities. RBAC implementation involves defining roles, assigning users to roles, and specifying permissions for each role. This process can be facilitated using IAM platforms or directory services that offer RBAC capabilities, such as Microsoft Active Directory (AD) or LDAP (Lightweight Directory Access Protocol) directories. In these systems, administrators can create role definitions, manage user-role assignments, and configure permissions through administrative interfaces or CLI commands. RBAC provides several benefits to organizations, including improved security posture, simplified access management, and enhanced compliance with regulatory requirements. By assigning access permissions based on job roles rather than individual users, RBAC reduces the risk of unauthorized access and data breaches, as users only have access to resources necessary for their roles. Moreover, RBAC streamlines access administration and audit processes, as changes to access permissions can be made centrally and applied consistently across the organization. RBAC also facilitates compliance with regulatory standards and industry best practices by enabling organizations to enforce least privilege principles and demonstrate adherence to access control policies. While RBAC offers significant advantages, its successful implementation requires careful planning, role design, and ongoing maintenance to ensure alignment with organizational needs and security objectives. Regular reviews of role definitions, user-role assignments, and permissions are essential to prevent access creep and maintain the integrity of access controls over time. Additionally, organizations may augment RBAC with other access control mechanisms, such as attribute-based access control (ABAC) or dynamic authorization, to address complex access requirements and support evolving business processes. By combining RBAC with complementary access control models and technologies, organizations can establish robust access management frameworks that effectively protect sensitive information assets and support business agility.

Chapter 5: Intrusion Detection and Prevention Protocols

Intrusion Detection Systems (IDS) are vital components of cybersecurity infrastructure, designed to monitor network and system activities for signs of unauthorized access, malicious activities, or security breaches. IDS play a crucial role in detecting and responding to cybersecurity threats in real-time, helping organizations safeguard their digital assets and maintain the integrity of their IT environments. IDS operate by analyzing network traffic, system logs, and other data sources to identify anomalous or suspicious behavior indicative of potential security incidents. There are two main types of IDS: network-based IDS (NIDS) and host-based IDS (HIDS). NIDS monitor network traffic flowing through routers, switches, and other network devices, inspecting packets for known attack signatures, abnormal patterns, or deviations from established baselines. HIDS, on the other hand, reside on individual hosts or endpoints, monitoring system logs, file integrity, and application activity to detect intrusions or unauthorized access attempts. To deploy an IDS effectively, organizations must first assess their cybersecurity requirements, infrastructure architecture, and risk profile to determine the most suitable IDS deployment strategy. This may involve deploying a combination of NIDS and HIDS solutions to provide comprehensive coverage across the network and endpoint environments. Once the deployment strategy is established, organizations can begin implementing the chosen IDS solutions and configuring them to align with their security policies and detection requirements. In a typical deployment scenario, NIDS sensors are strategically placed at key points within the network topology, such as perimeter gateways, internal network segments, and critical infrastructure components, to monitor inbound and outbound traffic for suspicious activity. NIDS sensors can be configured to analyze traffic at the packet level, examining header information, payload contents, and protocol behavior to detect known attack patterns or anomalous behavior. Common CLI commands used to configure NIDS sensors include commands to set up access control lists (ACLs), define intrusion detection policies, and configure alerting mechanisms for detected threats. Additionally, organizations may leverage network taps or span ports to facilitate passive monitoring of network traffic without disrupting network operations. In contrast, HIDS agents are deployed on individual hosts or endpoints to monitor system-level activities and detect signs of compromise or unauthorized access. HIDS agents can be installed on servers, workstations, or other critical assets to monitor file system changes, registry modifications, process activities, and user authentication events. CLI commands for configuring HIDS agents may include commands to install or update agent software, configure logging settings, and define monitoring rules for specific system resources or event types. Once deployed, IDS solutions continuously monitor network and system activities, generating alerts or alarms when suspicious behavior is detected. These alerts are typically sent to a centralized management console or security information and event management (SIEM) system for further analysis, correlation, and response. Administrators can then investigate the alerts, prioritize incidents based on severity and impact, and take appropriate remediation actions to mitigate the detected threats. Additionally, IDS solutions may support integration with other cybersecurity technologies, such as firewalls, antivirus software, and threat intelligence feeds, to enhance threat detection capabilities and facilitate automated response workflows. By deploying IDS solutions effectively and integrating them into broader cybersecurity frameworks, organizations can strengthen their defense-in-depth strategies, improve incident detection and response capabilities, and better protect their critical assets from evolving cyber threats.

Intrusion Prevention Systems (IPS) are critical components of modern cybersecurity defenses, designed to proactively identify and block malicious activities, exploits, and security threats before they can compromise network integrity or disrupt operations. IPS builds upon the capabilities of Intrusion Detection Systems (IDS) by not only detecting suspicious behavior but also taking automated action to prevent or mitigate potential security breaches. IPS operates by inspecting network traffic, system logs, and application activity in real-time, using a combination of signature-based detection, anomaly detection, and heuristic analysis techniques to identify and respond to potential threats. There are two primary deployment modes for IPS: in-line and out-of-band. In-line IPS solutions are deployed directly in the data path, allowing them to inspect and block traffic in real-time as it traverses the network. Out-of-band IPS solutions, on the other hand, operate passively, analyzing traffic copies or logs generated by network devices without directly impacting traffic flow. Deploying an IPS effectively requires careful planning, configuration, and tuning to ensure optimal performance and minimal impact on network operations. Organizations must first assess their security requirements, infrastructure architecture, and risk profile to determine the most appropriate IPS deployment strategy. This may involve deploying a combination of in-line and out-of-band IPS solutions to provide comprehensive coverage across different network segments and traffic types. Once the deployment strategy is established, organizations can begin implementing the chosen IPS solutions and configuring them to align with their security policies and threat detection requirements. In a typical deployment scenario, in-line IPS devices are strategically placed at key points within the network topology, such as perimeter gateways, internal network segments, and critical infrastructure components, to inspect inbound and outbound traffic for malicious activity. In-line IPS devices are configured to analyze traffic at wire speed, using predefined rulesets or custom signatures to detect and block known attacks, exploit attempts, or suspicious behavior. CLI commands for configuring in-line IPS devices may include commands to define traffic policies, configure rule sets, and enable specific protection mechanisms, such as intrusion prevention, protocol validation, or application layer inspection. Out-of-band IPS solutions, meanwhile, are deployed as passive sensors or analyzers, monitoring network traffic copies or logs generated by network devices to detect and analyze security events. Out-of-band

IPS devices can be deployed on dedicated hardware appliances, virtual machines, or cloud-based platforms, depending on the organization's infrastructure requirements and deployment preferences. CLI commands for configuring out-of-band IPS devices may include commands to set up traffic mirroring or spanning sessions, configure log collection and analysis settings, and define alerting thresholds for detected security events. Once deployed, IPS solutions continuously monitor network traffic and system activity, analyzing packets, sessions, and application payloads for signs of malicious behavior. When a potential threat is detected, IPS devices can take automated action to block or mitigate the threat in real-time, such as dropping malicious packets, terminating suspicious connections, or triggering alert notifications for further investigation. By deploying IPS solutions effectively and integrating them into broader cybersecurity frameworks, organizations can enhance their ability to detect, prevent, and respond to a wide range of cybersecurity threats, safeguarding their critical assets and maintaining the integrity of their IT environments.

Chapter 6: Firewalls and Firewall Protocols

Firewalls are essential components of network security infrastructure, acting as the first line of defense against unauthorized access, malicious traffic, and cyber threats. There are several types of firewalls, each with its unique features, capabilities, and deployment models. One of the most common types of firewalls is the stateful inspection firewall, which operates at the network layer of the OSI model and monitors the state of active connections to determine whether incoming packets should be allowed or denied based on predefined security policies. Another type of firewall is the application-layer firewall, also known as a proxy firewall, which operates at the application layer and inspects traffic at the application level, providing granular control over specific protocols and applications. Next, there are network-based firewalls, which are deployed as standalone appliances or software solutions within the network infrastructure, inspecting and filtering traffic as it flows between network segments or between the internal network and the Internet. Network-based firewalls are often configured using dedicated management interfaces or web-based administration consoles, where administrators can define access control rules, configure security policies, and monitor firewall activity in real-time. One popular network-based firewall solution is Cisco's Adaptive Security Appliance (ASA), which provides comprehensive firewalling, VPN, and intrusion prevention capabilities in a single integrated platform. CLI commands for configuring Cisco ASA firewalls may include commands to define access control lists (ACLs), configure NAT (Network Address Translation) policies, and enable security features such as stateful inspection and application-layer inspection. Another common type of firewall is the host-based firewall, which is installed on individual devices, such as servers, workstations, or mobile devices, to control inbound and outbound traffic at the operating system level. Host-based firewalls are often included as part of modern operating systems, such as Windows Firewall on Microsoft Windows or iptables on Linux, and can be configured using native management tools or third-party software solutions. CLI commands for configuring iptables on Linux may include commands to define firewall rules, specify source and destination addresses, and set up port forwarding or network address translation (NAT) rules. In addition to traditional firewalls, there are also next-generation firewalls (NGFWs), which integrate advanced security features such as intrusion prevention, application awareness, and deep packet inspection to provide enhanced protection against sophisticated cyber threats. NGFWs are designed to address the evolving threat landscape by combining traditional firewalling capabilities with advanced security technologies, such as threat intelligence feeds, behavioral analysis, and sandboxing, to detect and block a wide range of cyber threats in real-time. CLI commands for configuring NGFWs may include commands to define security policies, configure application-layer controls, and enable advanced threat protection features such as intrusion prevention systems (IPS), antivirus scanning, and URL filtering. Finally, there are also cloud-based firewalls, which are deployed as virtual appliances or software-as-a-service (SaaS) solutions within cloud environments to protect virtualized workloads, applications, and data hosted in the cloud. Cloud-based firewalls are designed to scale dynamically with cloud infrastructure and provide centralized management and policy enforcement across distributed environments.CLI commands for configuring cloud-based firewalls may vary depending on the specific cloud platform or service provider but typically involve commands to define security groups, configure network access control rules, and manage firewall policies through cloud management consoles or APIs. Firewall rule configuration and management are fundamental aspects of maintaining effective network security, enabling organizations to define and enforce access control policies that govern the flow of traffic to and from their networks. Firewall rules, also known as access control lists (ACLs), specify which types of traffic are allowed or denied based on criteria such as source and destination IP addresses, port numbers, and protocols. Configuring and managing firewall rules involves defining these rules, organizing them into rule sets, and regularly reviewing and updating them to adapt to changing security requirements and network conditions. One of the most common ways to configure firewall rules is through the command-line interface (CLI) of the firewall device or management software. For example, in Cisco ASA firewalls, administrators can use the "access-list" command to define access control rules, specifying parameters such as source and destination IP addresses, port numbers, and protocols, followed by the action to be taken (permit or deny). Similarly, in iptables on Linux systems, administrators can use commands such as "iptables -A INPUT" to append a new rule to the input chain, followed by parameters specifying the source and destination addresses, port numbers, and protocol, and the action to be taken (ACCEPT or DROP). When configuring firewall rules, it's essential to follow security best practices and adhere to the principle of least privilege, ensuring that only necessary traffic is allowed while blocking or restricting access to unauthorized or potentially malicious traffic. This involves carefully evaluating the requirements of the organization's applications, services, and users and defining firewall rules that reflect these requirements while minimizing the attack surface and potential security risks. In addition to defining basic access control rules, organizations may also implement more advanced firewall features and techniques to enhance security and control over network traffic. For example, stateful firewall inspection, which tracks the state of active connections and dynamically adjusts firewall rules to allow return traffic for established connections, can help prevent unauthorized access and protect against certain types of network attacks, such as denial-of-service (DoS) attacks or port scanning. Similarly, application-layer inspection, also known as deep packet inspection (DPI), allows firewalls to inspect and analyze the contents of application-layer protocols, such as HTTP, FTP, or DNS, enabling more granular control over specific types of traffic and the ability to detect and block malicious or unauthorized activities at the application level. When managing firewall rules, it's essential to maintain accurate documentation and records of rule sets, including details such as the purpose of each rule, the rationale behind its configuration, and any associated risk assessments or compliance requirements. This helps ensure transparency and accountability in the firewall rule management process and facilitates troubleshooting and auditing activities in the event of security incidents or compliance audits. Additionally, organizations should regularly review and update firewall rules to reflect changes in their network infrastructure, application landscape, and security posture. This may involve periodically reviewing firewall logs and traffic analysis reports to identify and address emerging threats or vulnerabilities, as well as conducting regular security assessments and penetration tests to validate the effectiveness of firewall configurations and identify potential gaps or weaknesses in security defenses. By following these best practices and adopting a proactive approach to firewall rule configuration and management, organizations can strengthen their overall security posture, mitigate risks, and better protect their networks, data, and assets from cyber threats and unauthorized access.

Chapter 7: Virtual Private Networks (VPNs) and Tunneling Protocols

VPN technologies and protocols play a crucial role in modern network security and remote access solutions, enabling organizations to establish secure connections over public networks such as the internet. Virtual Private Networks (VPNs) create encrypted tunnels between remote users or branch offices and a central network, allowing them to securely access resources and services as if they were directly connected to the private network. There are several VPN technologies and protocols available, each with its own strengths, weaknesses, and use cases. One of the most widely used VPN protocols is the Point-to-Point Tunneling Protocol (PPTP), which provides a simple and easy-to-deploy solution for establishing VPN connections. PPTP operates at the data link layer of the OSI model and uses a combination of Point-to-Point Protocol (PPP) authentication and Generic Routing Encapsulation (GRE) to encapsulate and encrypt VPN traffic. To configure a PPTP VPN server on a Linux system, administrators can use the "pptpd" daemon along with configuration files to specify parameters such as IP address ranges, authentication methods, and encryption settings. However, PPTP has known security vulnerabilities and is not considered secure for modern deployments, as it uses relatively weak encryption algorithms and has been compromised in the past. As a result, organizations are increasingly turning to more secure alternatives such as Layer 2 Tunneling Protocol (L2TP) and Internet Protocol Security (IPsec). L2TP/IPsec combines the features of L2TP for tunneling and IPsec for encryption and authentication, providing a more robust and secure VPN solution. L2TP/IPsec operates at the network layer of the OSI model and uses UDP port 500 for IKE (Internet Key Exchange) negotiation and IP protocol 50 for ESP (Encapsulating Security Payload) to encrypt data traffic. To configure an L2TP/IPsec VPN server on a Linux system, administrators can use the "xl2tpd" daemon for L2TP tunneling and the "strongSwan" or "Libreswan" IPsec implementation for encryption and authentication. Another popular VPN protocol is Secure Socket Tunneling Protocol (SSTP), which is developed by Microsoft and integrated into Windows operating systems. SSTP uses SSL/TLS encryption to secure VPN traffic over TCP port 443, making it firewall-friendly and suitable for bypassing network restrictions imposed by firewalls or proxies. To deploy an SSTP VPN server on a Windows Server system, administrators can use the Routing and Remote Access Services (RRAS) role along with a valid SSL certificate for securing connections. Additionally, organizations may opt for OpenVPN, an open-source VPN solution that offers flexibility, scalability, and strong security features. OpenVPN can operate in either point-to-point or site-to-site configurations and supports various encryption algorithms and authentication methods, including certificate-based authentication and multi-factor authentication. To set up an OpenVPN server, administrators can install the OpenVPN software package and configure server and client settings using configuration files and cryptographic keys generated by the "easy-rsa" utility. In addition to these traditional VPN protocols, newer technologies such as WireGuard are gaining popularity for their simplicity, performance, and security. WireGuard is a modern VPN protocol that aims to provide faster and more secure VPN connections with a smaller codebase and improved cryptographic primitives. Unlike traditional VPN protocols, WireGuard operates at the kernel level, making it lightweight and efficient while still offering strong encryption and authentication. To deploy a WireGuard VPN server, administrators can install the WireGuard software package and configure server and client settings using configuration files and cryptographic keys generated by the "wg" utility. Overall, VPN technologies and protocols play a vital role in securing network communications and enabling remote access for users and devices. By understanding the capabilities and characteristics of different VPN solutions, organizations can choose the most appropriate option based on their security requirements, performance needs, and deployment scenarios.

Tunneling protocols are essential components in network security architectures, providing secure communication channels over public or untrusted networks. These protocols encapsulate data packets within a secure tunnel, protecting them from interception and tampering by unauthorized parties. One of the most widely used tunneling protocols is the Point-to-Point Tunneling Protocol (PPTP), which enables the creation of virtual private networks (VPNs) for secure remote access. PPTP operates at the data link layer of the OSI model and is commonly deployed in Windows environments due to its native support. To configure a PPTP VPN server on a Windows Server system, administrators can use the "Routing and Remote Access" (RRAS) console or PowerShell commands to set up and manage VPN connections. However, PPTP has known security vulnerabilities, including weak encryption algorithms, and is not recommended for secure deployments. Another commonly used tunneling protocol is the Layer 2 Tunneling Protocol (L2TP), which provides enhanced security features compared to PPTP. L2TP operates at the data link layer and combines the features of PPTP with the security of the IPsec protocol suite. To deploy an L2TP/IPsec VPN server on a Linux system, administrators can use the "xl2tpd" daemon for L2TP tunneling and the "strongSwan" or "Libreswan" IPsec implementation for encryption and authentication. L2TP/IPsec is widely supported on various platforms, including Windows, macOS, iOS, and Android, making it suitable for cross-platform deployments. Internet Protocol Security (IPsec) is not a tunneling protocol itself but rather a suite of protocols used for securing IP communications. IPsec can be used in conjunction with tunneling protocols such as L2TP or IKEv2 to provide end-to-end encryption, data integrity, and authentication. To configure IPsec policies on a Linux system, administrators can use the "ip xfrm" and "setkey" commands to define security associations (SAs) and security policies. IPsec supports multiple encryption algorithms, hash functions, and authentication methods, allowing administrators to customize security settings according to their requirements. Additionally, IPsec can be deployed in transport mode for securing individual IP packets or tunnel mode for creating secure VPN connections between network endpoints. Secure Shell (SSH) is another tunneling protocol commonly used for secure remote access to network devices and servers. SSH operates at the application layer of the OSI model and provides encrypted communication channels for remote login, file transfer, and command execution. To establish an SSH session to a remote server or device, users can use the "ssh" command followed by the hostname or IP address of the target system. SSH supports various authentication methods, including password-based authentication, public key authentication, and multi-factor authentication, enhancing security and access control. Additionally, SSH can be configured to create dynamic port forwarding tunnels, allowing users to securely access internal network resources from remote locations. Overall, tunneling protocols play a crucial role in securing network communications and enabling secure remote access for users and devices. By understanding the capabilities and characteristics of different tunneling protocols, organizations can implement robust security solutions to protect their sensitive data and resources from unauthorized access and interception.

Chapter 8: Implementing Security Policies and Procedures

Security policies are foundational documents that outline an organization's guidelines, procedures, and best practices for protecting its information assets and infrastructure from security threats and vulnerabilities. These policies serve as a roadmap for establishing a robust security posture and ensuring compliance with regulatory requirements and industry standards. Developing effective security policies requires a comprehensive understanding of the organization's business objectives, risk tolerance, and regulatory environment. The process typically begins with a thorough risk assessment to identify potential security risks and vulnerabilities that could impact the organization's operations and reputation. Conducting a risk assessment involves evaluating the organization's assets, including hardware, software, data, and personnel, to determine their value and criticality to the business. Once the risk assessment is complete, the next step is to define the scope and objectives of the security policies. This involves identifying the specific areas of security that need to be addressed, such as data protection, access control, incident response, and compliance. With the scope and objectives established, the organization can then proceed to develop the actual security policies. This process involves drafting policy documents that clearly articulate the organization's expectations regarding security practices and procedures. Each policy should be written in clear and concise language, avoiding technical jargon and ambiguity to ensure understanding and compliance by all stakeholders. Additionally, security policies should be tailored to the organization's unique needs and requirements, taking into account factors such as industry regulations, business operations, and technological infrastructure. For example, an organization operating in the healthcare sector may need to develop specific policies related to patient privacy and data security to comply with regulations such as the Health Insurance Portability and Accountability Act (HIPAA). Similarly, a financial institution may need to establish policies for securing customer financial information in accordance with the Payment Card Industry Data Security Standard (PCI DSS). As part of the policy development process, organizations should also consider the input and feedback of key stakeholders, including senior management, IT staff, legal counsel, and regulatory compliance experts. Collaboration among these stakeholders ensures that the policies are comprehensive, enforceable, and aligned with the organization's strategic objectives. Once the policies have been drafted, they should undergo a review and approval process to ensure accuracy, completeness, and adherence to relevant standards and regulations. This may involve legal review to ensure compliance with applicable laws and regulations, as well as technical review to assess the feasibility and effectiveness of proposed security measures. After the policies have been approved, they should be communicated to all relevant stakeholders within the organization. This typically involves conducting training sessions or awareness programs to educate employees about their roles and responsibilities in maintaining security. Additionally, organizations may use various communication channels, such as email, intranet portals, and employee handbooks, to disseminate the policies and ensure widespread awareness. It is also important to regularly review and update security policies to reflect changes in the organization's business environment, technology landscape, and regulatory requirements. This ensures that the policies remain relevant and effective in addressing emerging security threats and evolving business needs. Finally, organizations should establish mechanisms for monitoring and enforcing compliance with security policies. This may involve implementing technical controls, such as access controls, encryption, and intrusion detection systems, to enforce policy requirements and detect violations. Additionally, organizations should establish procedures for responding to policy violations, including disciplinary actions, remediation measures, and incident response protocols. By following these best practices for developing and implementing security policies, organizations can strengthen their security posture, protect their information assets, and mitigate the risks associated with cyber threats and data breaches.

Security policy enforcement and compliance are critical aspects of maintaining a robust cybersecurity posture within an organization's IT infrastructure, ensuring that established security policies are effectively implemented and adhered to by all users and devices. Enforcement mechanisms play a vital role in preventing security breaches, protecting sensitive data, and mitigating potential risks associated with unauthorized access or malicious activity. One of the fundamental methods for enforcing security policies is through the use of access control mechanisms, which regulate user access to resources based on predefined rules and permissions. Access control lists (ACLs) are commonly used in network devices such as routers, switches, and firewalls to restrict or allow traffic based on criteria such as source and destination IP addresses, port numbers, and protocols. For example, in a Cisco router, the "access-list" command is used to create an ACL, and the "permit" or "deny" statements are used to define specific traffic conditions. Once the ACL is configured, it can be applied to an interface using the "ip access-group" command, effectively enforcing the specified security policies. In addition to access control, encryption technologies play a crucial role in enforcing security policies, especially when transmitting sensitive data over insecure networks. Transport Layer Security (TLS) and Secure Sockets Layer (SSL) protocols are widely used to encrypt data communications between clients and servers, ensuring confidentiality and integrity. To enforce encryption policies, organizations can deploy TLS/SSL certificates issued by trusted certificate authorities (CAs) to authenticate servers and establish secure connections. In a web server environment, administrators can use tools like OpenSSL to generate certificate signing requests (CSRs), which can then be submitted to a CA for signing. Once the certificate is obtained, it can be installed on the server along with the private key to enable TLS/SSL encryption. Compliance monitoring and auditing are essential components of security policy enforcement, providing organizations with visibility into their security posture and identifying areas of non-compliance or potential vulnerabilities. Security Information and Event Management (SIEM) systems are commonly used to collect, correlate, and analyze security events and log data from various sources, including network devices, servers, and applications. SIEM platforms enable organizations to define security policies and rules for detecting suspicious activity or policy violations, such as unauthorized access attempts, malware infections, or data breaches. By monitoring SIEM alerts and reports, security teams can identify security incidents in real-time and take appropriate actions to remediate them, such as blocking malicious IP addresses, quarantining infected devices, or applying security patches. Continuous compliance monitoring is essential for ensuring that security policies remain effective and up-to-date in response to evolving threats and regulatory requirements. Automated compliance management solutions can streamline the process of assessing and enforcing security policies by scanning IT infrastructure for compliance with industry standards and regulatory frameworks, such as the Payment Card Industry Data Security Standard (PCI DSS), Health Insurance Portability and Accountability Act (HIPAA), or General Data Protection Regulation (GDPR). These solutions can generate compliance reports, identify areas of non-compliance, and recommend remediation actions to address security gaps and vulnerabilities. In addition to technical controls, security policy enforcement also relies on organizational measures such as security awareness training, employee education, and regular security audits and assessments. By fostering a culture of security awareness and accountability, organizations can empower employees to recognize and report security threats, adhere to security best practices, and comply with established security policies and procedures. Ultimately, effective security policy enforcement and compliance are essential for protecting organizations against cyber threats, minimizing the risk of data breaches, and maintaining trust and confidence in the integrity and confidentiality of their information assets.

Chapter 9: Network Security Auditing and Monitoring

Auditing tools and techniques play a crucial role in ensuring the security and integrity of IT systems and networks by providing organizations with the means to assess, monitor, and analyze their infrastructure for compliance with security policies, regulatory requirements, and industry best practices. These tools encompass a wide range of capabilities, including vulnerability scanning, configuration auditing, log analysis, and compliance management, designed to identify potential security risks, vulnerabilities, and weaknesses within an organization's IT environment. One of the fundamental auditing techniques is vulnerability scanning, which involves the use of automated tools to scan network devices, servers, and applications for known vulnerabilities and misconfigurations that could be exploited by attackers. Vulnerability scanners such as Nessus, OpenVAS, and Qualys are commonly used to perform comprehensive scans of IT infrastructure, identifying security flaws such as missing patches, outdated software versions, weak passwords, and insecure configurations. The output of vulnerability scans typically includes detailed reports outlining identified vulnerabilities, their severity levels, and recommendations for remediation. In addition to vulnerability scanning, configuration auditing is another essential technique for assessing the security posture of IT systems and ensuring compliance with security standards and policies. Configuration auditing tools such as Tripwire and Nipper are used to compare the current configuration of network devices, servers, and applications against predefined security baselines or industry best practices, identifying deviations from expected configurations that could pose security risks. These tools help organizations enforce security policies, detect unauthorized changes, and maintain the integrity and consistency of their IT infrastructure. Log analysis is another critical auditing technique that involves monitoring and analyzing system logs, event logs, and audit trails generated by various IT components to detect security incidents, suspicious activities, and policy violations. Security Information and Event Management (SIEM) solutions such as Splunk, LogRhythm, and IBM QRadar are widely used for centralized log management, correlation, and analysis, enabling organizations to aggregate, normalize, and correlate log data from multiple sources to detect security threats and anomalies. SIEM platforms provide real-time monitoring capabilities, customizable dashboards, and alerting mechanisms to help security teams quickly identify and respond to security incidents. Compliance management is an essential aspect of auditing, ensuring that organizations adhere to regulatory requirements, industry standards, and internal security policies. Compliance management tools such as Tenable.sc, Qualys Policy Compliance, and McAfee Policy Auditor help organizations assess their compliance posture, automate compliance assessments, and generate audit reports for regulatory audits and certifications. These tools enable organizations to define and enforce security policies, track compliance status, and demonstrate compliance with regulatory mandates to auditors and stakeholders. Penetration testing, also known as ethical hacking, is a proactive auditing technique that involves simulating real-world cyber attacks to identify security weaknesses and vulnerabilities in an organization's IT infrastructure. Penetration testing tools such as Metasploit, Nmap, and Burp Suite are used by certified ethical hackers (CEHs) and security professionals to perform controlled attacks against target systems, uncovering security flaws that could be exploited by malicious actors. By conducting penetration tests regularly, organizations can identify and remediate security vulnerabilities before they can be exploited by attackers, reducing the risk of data breaches and security incidents. Continuous monitoring and auditing are essential for maintaining the effectiveness of security controls, detecting emerging threats, and ensuring ongoing compliance with security policies and regulations. By leveraging auditing tools and techniques, organizations can proactively identify and mitigate security risks, strengthen their security posture, and protect their valuable assets from cyber threats.

Continuous monitoring strategies are essential components of modern cybersecurity practices, providing organizations with real-time visibility into their IT infrastructure, detecting security threats, and ensuring compliance with regulatory requirements and security policies. These strategies involve the continuous collection, analysis, and interpretation of security-related data from various sources, including network devices, servers, applications, and user activities. By monitoring key performance indicators (KPIs), security events, and system logs, organizations can identify potential security incidents, unauthorized activities, and compliance violations promptly. One of the fundamental aspects of continuous monitoring is the use of security information and event management (SIEM) solutions, which centralize log data from diverse sources, correlate events, and generate alerts for suspicious activities. SIEM platforms such as Splunk, IBM QRadar, and LogRhythm collect log data from firewalls, intrusion detection systems (IDS), antivirus software, and other security tools, enabling security teams to analyze security events in real-time and respond to incidents effectively. To deploy a SIEM solution, organizations typically install and configure the SIEM software on dedicated servers or virtual machines, configure data sources to forward logs to the SIEM platform, and create custom rules and alerts based on security policies and requirements. Another critical component of continuous monitoring is network traffic analysis, which involves the inspection and analysis of network packets to identify abnormal or malicious activities. Network traffic analysis tools such as Wireshark, Suricata, and Bro provide deep packet inspection capabilities, allowing security analysts to monitor network traffic, detect potential threats, and investigate security incidents. By capturing and analyzing network packets in real-time, organizations can identify unauthorized access attempts, malware infections, and data exfiltration attempts, mitigating security risks and preventing data breaches. Deploying network traffic analysis tools involves installing the software on dedicated monitoring servers or network appliances, configuring network interfaces to capture traffic, and setting up filters and rules to analyze traffic patterns and detect anomalies. Endpoint monitoring is another essential aspect of continuous monitoring, focusing on the security of individual devices such as desktops, laptops, servers, and mobile devices. Endpoint monitoring solutions such as CrowdStrike, Carbon Black, and Symantec Endpoint Protection provide real-time visibility into endpoint activities, detect malicious behavior, and block threats at the endpoint level. By monitoring endpoint activities, organizations can detect and respond to malware infections, insider threats, and endpoint vulnerabilities promptly. Deploying endpoint monitoring solutions involves installing agent software on endpoint devices, configuring policies to monitor endpoint activities, and integrating with other security tools for centralized management and response. Continuous vulnerability scanning is a critical practice for identifying and remediating security vulnerabilities in IT systems and applications. Vulnerability scanning tools such as Nessus, OpenVAS, and Qualys Vulnerability Management automate the process of scanning IT infrastructure for known vulnerabilities, misconfigurations, and security weaknesses. By conducting regular vulnerability scans, organizations can identify and prioritize security vulnerabilities for remediation, reducing the risk of cyber attacks and data breaches. Deploying vulnerability scanning tools involves installing and configuring the scanning software on dedicated servers or appliances, scheduling regular scans of network devices, servers, and applications, and analyzing scan results to identify and prioritize vulnerabilities. Continuous monitoring also involves the use of threat intelligence feeds and security analytics to enhance threat detection capabilities and improve incident response effectiveness. Threat intelligence feeds provide organizations with timely information about emerging threats, malicious actors, and attack techniques, enabling them to proactively defend against cyber threats. Security analytics platforms such as Cisco Stealthwatch, RSA NetWitness, and FireEye Helix analyze security data from multiple sources, including SIEM logs, network traffic, and endpoint activities, to detect advanced threats and suspicious behavior. By leveraging threat intelligence feeds and security analytics, organizations can enhance their situational awareness, identify indicators of compromise (IOCs), and respond to security incidents more effectively. In summary, continuous monitoring strategies are essential for maintaining the security and resilience of modern IT environments, enabling organizations to detect and respond to security threats in real-time, ensure compliance with regulatory requirements, and protect their valuable assets from cyber attacks. By leveraging advanced monitoring tools, threat intelligence feeds, and security analytics, organizations can enhance their security posture, mitigate risks, and safeguard against evolving cyber threats.

Chapter 10: Incident Response and Disaster Recovery Protocols

Incident response planning and execution are critical components of cybersecurity preparedness, ensuring organizations can effectively detect, respond to, and recover from security incidents and data breaches. Incident response planning involves the development of comprehensive strategies, policies, and procedures to guide the organization's response to security incidents, including data breaches, malware infections, unauthorized access attempts, and denial-of-service (DoS) attacks. The incident response plan outlines roles and responsibilities, escalation procedures, communication protocols, and mitigation strategies to minimize the impact of security incidents on the organization's operations and reputation. One of the first steps in incident response planning is to establish an incident response team comprised of individuals with diverse skills and expertise in cybersecurity, IT operations, legal, and communications. The incident response team is responsible for coordinating the organization's response to security incidents, assessing the severity and impact of incidents, and implementing remediation measures to contain and mitigate the damage. To deploy an incident response team, organizations typically designate team members, define their roles and responsibilities, and conduct regular training and tabletop exercises to ensure readiness and effectiveness. Incident response planning also involves the development of incident response playbooks, which are detailed guides that outline step-by-step procedures for responding to specific types of security incidents. Incident response playbooks include predefined actions, decision trees, and checklists to guide responders through the incident detection, analysis, containment, eradication, and recovery phases. By creating incident response playbooks, organizations can streamline their response efforts, reduce response times, and ensure consistency in incident handling across the organization. Deploying incident response playbooks involves documenting incident response procedures, validating the procedures through tabletop exercises and simulations, and updating the playbooks regularly to reflect changes in the threat landscape and technology environment. Incident detection and analysis are critical aspects of incident response, enabling organizations to identify and assess security incidents promptly. Incident detection involves the monitoring of security events, logs, and alerts from various sources, including network devices, servers, applications, and security tools. Security information and event management (SIEM) solutions such as Splunk, IBM QRadar, and LogRhythm aggregate and correlate security event data from disparate sources, enabling organizations to detect anomalous activities and potential security incidents in real-time. Deploying a SIEM solution involves configuring data sources to forward logs to the SIEM platform, creating custom rules and alerts to detect suspicious activities, and configuring dashboards and reports to visualize security events and trends. Incident analysis involves investigating security incidents to determine their cause, scope, and impact on the organization's systems and data. Security analysts use various techniques and tools to analyze security event data, including log analysis, packet capture analysis, malware analysis, and forensic analysis. Log analysis involves reviewing system and application logs to identify abnormal or suspicious activities, such as unauthorized access attempts, unusual login patterns, and system errors. Packet capture analysis involves capturing and analyzing network traffic to identify malicious or anomalous network behavior, such as network scanning, data exfiltration, and command-and-control communications. Malware analysis involves analyzing malware samples to understand their behavior, functionality, and impact on infected systems. Forensic analysis involves collecting and preserving digital evidence from compromised systems, such as disk images, memory dumps, and network traffic captures, to support incident investigations and legal proceedings. Incident containment and eradication are crucial steps in incident response, aiming to limit the damage caused by security incidents and prevent further compromise of the organization's systems and data. Incident containment involves isolating affected systems, networks, or applications to prevent the spread of malware, unauthorized access, or data leakage. Depending on the nature and severity of the incident, containment measures may include disabling compromised accounts, blocking malicious IP addresses, disconnecting infected systems from the network, and implementing firewall rules to restrict traffic. Incident eradication involves removing the root cause of the incident from the organization's systems and restoring them to a secure and operational state. This may involve removing malware infections, patching vulnerabilities, restoring data from backups, and implementing security controls to prevent similar incidents in the future. Incident recovery is the final phase of the incident response process, focusing on restoring the organization's systems, operations, and data to normalcy after a security incident. Incident recovery involves recovering and restoring affected systems and data from backups, verifying the integrity and functionality of restored systems, and implementing additional security measures to prevent recurrence of the incident. Additionally, organizations may conduct post-incident reviews and lessons learned sessions to evaluate the effectiveness of their incident response efforts, identify areas for improvement, and update their incident response plans and procedures accordingly. By continuously refining their incident response capabilities and practices, organizations can enhance their resilience to security threats and minimize the impact of security incidents on their operations and reputation. Disaster recovery protocols and contingency plans are essential components of an organization's cybersecurity and business continuity strategies, aimed at minimizing the impact of unforeseen events such as natural disasters, cyber attacks, hardware failures, and human errors on its operations and services. These protocols and plans outline a systematic approach to recovering critical systems, applications, and data following a disruptive event, ensuring that the organization can resume normal operations as quickly and efficiently as possible. To deploy disaster recovery protocols and contingency plans effectively, organizations must first conduct a comprehensive risk assessment to identify potential threats and vulnerabilities that could disrupt their business operations. This involves analyzing various factors such as geographical location, infrastructure dependencies, regulatory requirements, and the likelihood of different types of disasters. Following the risk assessment, organizations can develop tailored disaster recovery plans that outline specific procedures and strategies for responding to different types of disruptive events. These plans typically include predefined steps for assessing the severity of the incident, activating the appropriate response teams, and initiating recovery efforts. One of the key elements of disaster recovery planning is establishing recovery time objectives (RTOs) and recovery point objectives (RPOs) for critical systems and services. RTOs define the maximum acceptable downtime for restoring operations after a disaster, while RPOs specify the maximum acceptable data loss in the event of a disruption. By defining RTOs and RPOs, organizations can prioritize their recovery efforts and allocate resources more effectively. Deploying disaster recovery protocols involves implementing a combination of technological solutions, operational procedures, and organizational measures to ensure business continuity and resilience in the face of adversity. One common technology used in disaster recovery is data replication, which involves copying data from primary systems to secondary or remote locations in real-time or near-real-time. This ensures that organizations have redundant copies of their data that can be quickly accessed and restored in the event of a disaster. CLI commands such as rsync or scp can be used to synchronize data between primary and secondary storage systems, while storage replication technologies such as synchronous or asynchronous replication can automate the process of copying data between geographically dispersed locations. In addition to data replication, organizations may also implement backup and restore solutions to protect their critical data and applications from loss or corruption. Backup solutions such as rsnapshot or BackupPC create regular backups of data and store them in secure locations, allowing organizations to restore data to a previous state in the event of data loss or corruption. Similarly, restore solutions such as tar or rsync can be used to recover data from backups and restore it to its original location. Alongside technological solutions, organizations must also establish clear procedures and protocols for activating and executing their disaster recovery plans. This involves defining roles and responsibilities for key personnel, establishing communication channels for coordinating response efforts, and conducting regular training and drills to ensure that staff are familiar with their roles and responsibilities during a crisis. By practicing their disaster recovery procedures regularly, organizations can identify weaknesses or gaps in their plans and make necessary adjustments to improve their effectiveness. Moreover, organizations must also consider the regulatory and compliance requirements that may impact their disaster recovery planning and execution. Depending on the industry and geographic location, organizations may be subject to various regulatory mandates that dictate specific requirements for disaster recovery and business continuity. For example, the Health Insurance Portability and Accountability Act (HIPAA) in the United States requires healthcare organizations to have contingency plans in place to protect sensitive patient data and ensure continuity of care during emergencies. Similarly, the Payment Card Industry Data Security Standard (PCI DSS) mandates that organizations that process credit card payments have robust disaster recovery plans to safeguard cardholder data and maintain uninterrupted service availability. Compliance with these regulations requires organizations to not only develop comprehensive disaster recovery plans but also regularly test and validate their effectiveness through audits and assessments. In summary, disaster recovery protocols and contingency plans are essential components of an organization's cybersecurity and business continuity strategies, providing a framework for responding to and recovering from disruptive events. By deploying a combination of technological solutions, operational procedures, and organizational measures, organizations can minimize the impact of disasters on their operations and ensure the continuity of critical services. Moreover, regular testing, training, and compliance with regulatory requirements are essential to ensuring the effectiveness and reliability of disaster recovery plans in real-world scenarios.

BOOK 4

ADVANCED PROTOCOL DYNAMICS

DELVING INTO COMPLEX NETWORK COMMUNICATION STRATEGIES

ROB BOTWRIGHT

Chapter 1: Advanced Routing Protocols and Strategies

Dynamic routing protocols play a crucial role in modern computer networks, facilitating the automatic exchange of routing information between routers to adapt to changes in network topology and traffic patterns. These protocols enable routers to dynamically discover the best path to reach a destination based on metrics such as hop count, bandwidth, delay, and reliability. One of the most widely used dynamic routing protocols is the Routing Information Protocol (RIP), which operates based on the distance-vector algorithm and is commonly used in small to medium-sized networks. RIP periodically broadcasts routing updates containing information about reachable networks to neighboring routers, allowing them to update their routing tables accordingly. However, RIP has limitations in terms of scalability and convergence speed, making it less suitable for large and complex networks. Another popular dynamic routing protocol is the Open Shortest Path First (OSPF) protocol, which uses a link-state algorithm to calculate the shortest path to each destination based on the network topology. OSPF routers exchange link-state advertisements (LSAs) to build a complete map of the network, allowing them to calculate optimal routes using the Dijkstra algorithm. OSPF is well-suited for large enterprise networks and Internet Service Provider (ISP) environments due to its fast convergence and support for hierarchical network design. To deploy OSPF, administrators configure OSPF-enabled routers with the appropriate OSPF router ID, area assignments, and authentication settings using commands such as router ospf, network, area, and authentication. OSPF routers establish adjacencies with neighboring routers in the same area and exchange LSAs to build a complete picture of the network topology. OSPF calculates the shortest path to each destination based on the cost associated with each link and installs these routes in the routing table. OSPF also supports features such as route summarization, route redistribution, and virtual links, making it highly flexible and adaptable to various network requirements. Additionally, Enhanced Interior Gateway Routing Protocol (EIGRP) is another dynamic routing protocol developed by Cisco Systems, combining the best aspects of distance-vector and link-state algorithms. EIGRP routers exchange routing updates using Reliable Transport Protocol (RTP) and build a topology table containing information about all known routes in the network. EIGRP uses a hybrid metric that considers bandwidth, delay, reliability, and load when calculating the best path to a destination. EIGRP is widely used in Cisco-based networks due to its efficient use of bandwidth and fast convergence times. Deploying EIGRP involves configuring routers with the appropriate EIGRP autonomous system number (ASN) and enabling EIGRP on interfaces using commands such as router eigrp and network. EIGRP routers establish neighbor adjacencies and exchange routing information to build their topology tables and calculate optimal routes. EIGRP supports features such as route summarization, unequal-cost load balancing, and stub routing, providing administrators with granular control over routing behavior. Additionally, Border Gateway Protocol (BGP) is a dynamic routing protocol commonly used in large-scale networks such as the Internet to exchange routing information between autonomous systems. Unlike interior gateway protocols like OSPF and EIGRP, which operate within a single administrative domain, BGP is an exterior gateway protocol that enables routers in different autonomous systems to exchange reachability information. BGP routers establish peer relationships with neighboring routers and exchange routing updates containing information about IP prefixes and their associated attributes. To deploy BGP, administrators configure BGP routers with the appropriate BGP autonomous system number (ASN) and establish peer connections using commands such as router bgp and neighbor. BGP routers exchange routing information and use policy-based routing decisions to determine the best path to reach each destination. BGP supports advanced features such as route aggregation, route filtering, and route reflectors, making it highly scalable and flexible. In summary, dynamic routing protocols play a vital role in modern computer networks by enabling routers to dynamically adapt to changes in network topology and traffic patterns. RIP, OSPF, EIGRP, and BGP are among the most commonly used dynamic routing protocols, each offering unique features and capabilities to meet the diverse needs of different network environments. Deploying dynamic routing protocols involves configuring routers with the appropriate protocol settings and establishing neighbor adjacencies to exchange routing information effectively.

Routing protocol optimization techniques are essential for improving the efficiency, stability, and performance of routing protocols in computer networks. These techniques aim to enhance the convergence speed, reduce routing overhead, and optimize the routing decision-making process. One common optimization technique is route summarization, which involves aggregating multiple network prefixes into a single summarized route advertisement. By reducing the number of routing entries in the routing table, route summarization helps minimize the size of routing updates and decreases the amount of memory and processing power required by routers to maintain their routing tables. Route summarization can be implemented using commands such as ip summary-address in Cisco IOS devices or by configuring summary routes in the routing protocol configuration. Another optimization technique is route filtering, which allows network administrators to control the propagation of routing information based on specific criteria. Route filtering can be used to prevent the advertisement of certain routes, limit the scope of route advertisements to specific interfaces or neighbors, or modify route attributes before propagation. This technique helps reduce unnecessary routing information exchange and prevents the propagation of incorrect or malicious routing updates. Route filtering can be implemented using access control lists (ACLs) or prefix lists in Cisco IOS devices, or by using route maps to apply filtering policies selectively. Additionally, route dampening is a technique used to suppress the impact of unstable routes on routing protocol convergence. When a route flaps frequently due to network instability or routing protocol instability, route dampening temporarily suppresses the advertisement of the route to prevent it from causing unnecessary routing instability. Route dampening assigns a penalty score to routes based on their stability, and routes with high penalty scores are suppressed for a configurable period. Route dampening can be configured in routing protocols such as BGP using commands like neighbor route-map or bgp dampening. Another optimization technique is equal-cost multipath (ECMP) routing, which allows routers to distribute traffic across multiple equal-cost paths to the same destination. By load balancing traffic across multiple paths, ECMP improves network performance, reduces congestion, and enhances fault tolerance. ECMP is commonly used in interior routing protocols such as OSPF and EIGRP, where routers maintain multiple equal-cost routes to the same destination and forward packets based on a hash of packet header information. ECMP can be configured by enabling it in the routing protocol configuration and ensuring that routers have multiple equal-cost paths to the destination network. Additionally, protocol-specific optimization techniques can be applied to improve the performance of specific routing protocols. For example, tuning parameters such as timers, hello intervals, and dead intervals can optimize the convergence speed and stability of routing protocols. Similarly, configuring authentication mechanisms, such as MD5 authentication for OSPF or BGP, can enhance the security of routing protocol exchanges and prevent unauthorized route injection. Moreover, implementing route summarization, route filtering, route dampening, ECMP, and protocol-specific optimizations can significantly improve the efficiency and stability of routing protocols in computer networks. By optimizing routing protocol operation, network administrators can ensure reliable and efficient communication within their networks while minimizing the impact of network failures and congestion.

Chapter 2: Scalability and Load Balancing Protocols

Scalability challenges in networking arise due to the increasing complexity and size of modern networks, which demand robust solutions to accommodate growth while maintaining performance and reliability. One of the key scalability challenges is addressing the exponential growth of network traffic driven by the proliferation of connected devices, the rise of data-intensive applications, and the increasing adoption of cloud services. As network traffic volume grows, traditional networking equipment and architectures may struggle to handle the increased load efficiently, leading to congestion, latency, and degraded performance. To address these challenges, network architects and administrators must adopt scalable network designs and technologies capable of handling large volumes of traffic while ensuring optimal performance. One approach to improving network scalability is the deployment of high-speed network infrastructure, such as 10 Gigabit Ethernet (10GbE) or 40 Gigabit Ethernet (40GbE) switches and routers, which provide greater bandwidth capacity to accommodate growing traffic demands. By upgrading to higher-speed networking equipment, organizations can increase their network capacity and support more devices and applications without sacrificing performance. Additionally, the adoption of modular and distributed network architectures can enhance scalability by allowing network resources to be dynamically allocated and scaled based on demand. Modular architectures, such as spine-and-leaf or fabric-based designs, enable organizations to add additional network capacity and redundancy by simply adding more modules or nodes to the existing infrastructure. These architectures provide flexibility and scalability while minimizing downtime and disruption to network operations. Virtualization technologies also play a critical role in addressing scalability challenges by decoupling network services from underlying hardware and enabling the dynamic allocation of resources based on demand. Technologies such as virtual LANs (VLANs), virtual routing and forwarding (VRF), and virtual private networks (VPNs) allow organizations to create logical network segments and services that can be scaled independently of physical infrastructure. Moreover, the adoption of software-defined networking (SDN) and network functions virtualization (NFV) further enhances scalability by centralizing network management and control functions and enabling automated provisioning and orchestration of network resources. SDN architectures, such as OpenFlow, separate the control plane from the data plane, allowing network administrators to centrally manage network policies and configurations from a single controller. NFV enables organizations to virtualize and abstract network functions, such as firewalls, load balancers, and intrusion detection systems, into software-based instances that can be deployed and scaled dynamically. Another scalability challenge in networking is ensuring robust security and access controls to protect against cyber threats and unauthorized access. As networks grow in size and complexity, they become increasingly susceptible to security breaches and attacks, making it essential to implement scalable security solutions that can defend against evolving threats. Technologies such as next-generation firewalls (NGFWs), intrusion prevention systems (IPS), and security information and event management (SIEM) platforms provide advanced threat detection and mitigation capabilities to safeguard network assets and data. Additionally, the adoption of zero-trust security models and microsegmentation strategies can enhance scalability by restricting access to network resources based on user identity, device posture, and application context. By implementing granular access controls and segmentation policies, organizations can limit the blast radius of security incidents and prevent lateral movement by attackers within the network. Furthermore, scalability challenges extend beyond technical considerations to include operational and organizational factors such as resource management, skill gaps, and budget constraints. Effective network scalability requires collaboration between network engineers, IT administrators, and business stakeholders to align technology investments with organizational goals and priorities. Additionally, ongoing monitoring, performance tuning, and capacity planning are essential to ensure that network resources remain optimized and scalable as requirements evolve over time. In summary, addressing scalability challenges in networking requires a holistic approach that combines technology innovation, best practices, and collaboration to build resilient, high-performance networks capable of supporting the growing demands of modern business environments. By adopting scalable network architectures, virtualization technologies, security solutions, and operational practices, organizations can overcome scalability challenges and position themselves for future growth and success. Load balancing algorithms and protocols play a crucial role in distributing network traffic across multiple servers or resources to optimize performance, maximize availability, and ensure scalability in modern network environments. One of the most common load balancing algorithms is

Round Robin, which evenly distributes incoming requests among a pool of servers in a sequential manner. In Round Robin, each new request is directed to the next server in the list, ensuring a balanced distribution of traffic. This algorithm is simple to implement and does not require complex configuration, making it suitable for basic load balancing requirements. However, Round Robin may not be ideal for environments with heterogeneous server capacities or variable workload characteristics, as it does not take into account server load or response times. To address these limitations, weighted round-robin (WRR) load balancing assigns a weight to each server based on its capacity or performance, allowing more traffic to be directed to higher-capacity servers. WRR ensures that servers with greater processing power or bandwidth receive a larger share of the incoming requests, leading to more efficient resource utilization and improved performance. Another popular load balancing algorithm is Least Connections, which directs incoming requests to the server with the fewest active connections at the time of the request. By prioritizing servers with the lowest connection count, Least Connections ensures that new requests are evenly distributed among the available resources, preventing overloading of individual servers and minimizing response times. This algorithm is well-suited for environments with dynamic workload patterns or fluctuating traffic volumes, as it adapts to changes in server load in real time. However, Least Connections may not be suitable for environments with long-lived connections or persistent sessions, as it does not take into account server capacity or performance metrics. To address this limitation, weighted least connections (WLC) load balancing assigns a weight to each server based on its capacity or performance, similar to WRR, but directs traffic to the server with the fewest active connections weighted by server capacity. This approach ensures that servers with higher capacity receive a larger share of the incoming requests, leading to more efficient resource utilization and improved performance. Another important load balancing algorithm is Least Response Time, which directs incoming requests to the server with the shortest response time based on historical performance metrics or real-time monitoring data. By prioritizing servers with the fastest response times, Least Response Time ensures that new requests are served by the most responsive resources, minimizing latency and improving user experience. This algorithm is particularly effective in environments with heterogeneous server capacities or variable workload characteristics, as it dynamically adapts to changes in server performance and network conditions. However,

Least Response Time may require more complex monitoring and measurement mechanisms to accurately assess server response times and make optimal routing decisions. In addition to these traditional load balancing algorithms, modern load balancers often employ more advanced techniques such as content-based routing, predictive analytics, and machine learning to optimize traffic distribution and improve application performance. Content-based routing allows load balancers to inspect the content of incoming requests and route them to the most appropriate server based on predefined criteria such as URL path, request headers, or payload content. This enables more granular traffic management and can improve application performance by ensuring that requests are directed to servers with the necessary processing capabilities or cached content. Predictive analytics and machine learning algorithms analyze historical traffic patterns, server performance metrics, and other relevant data to predict future workload demands and optimize load balancing decisions in real time. By proactively adjusting traffic distribution based on predictive models and trend analysis, these techniques can help prevent performance bottlenecks, optimize resource utilization, and improve overall system efficiency. In summary, load balancing algorithms and protocols are essential components of modern network infrastructure, enabling organizations to efficiently distribute traffic, maximize resource utilization, and enhance application performance. By understanding the strengths and limitations of different load balancing techniques and selecting the most appropriate algorithms for their specific requirements, organizations can build scalable, resilient, and high-performance networks that meet the evolving demands of their users and applications.

Chapter 3: Multicast and Anycast Protocols

Multicast routing protocols are fundamental to efficiently distributing data packets from one source to multiple destinations within a network, facilitating bandwidth conservation and minimizing network congestion. One of the most widely used multicast routing protocols is Protocol Independent Multicast (PIM), which operates at the network layer of the OSI model and enables routers to efficiently forward multicast traffic. PIM is designed to work in both dense and sparse multicast environments, making it suitable for a wide range of network topologies and applications. In a dense mode environment, PIM floods multicast packets to all routers within a multicast group, allowing routers to quickly establish a multicast distribution tree and forward packets to all group members. However, dense mode may not be efficient in networks with a sparse distribution of group members or limited bandwidth, as it can lead to unnecessary traffic replication and network congestion. To address this limitation, PIM also supports sparse mode operation, where routers only forward multicast packets along branches of the multicast tree where group members are located, conserving bandwidth and minimizing unnecessary traffic propagation. Another commonly used multicast routing protocol is the Multicast Open Shortest Path First (MOSPF) protocol, which extends the OSPF routing protocol to support multicast routing. MOSPF builds multicast distribution trees based on the existing unicast routing topology established by OSPF, leveraging OSPF's link-state routing algorithm to compute optimal paths for multicast traffic. By integrating multicast routing with unicast routing, MOSPF simplifies network management and ensures consistency between unicast and multicast forwarding paths. However, MOSPF may not be as scalable as PIM in large-scale multicast environments, as it relies on the flooding of Link State Advertisements (LSAs) to propagate multicast routing information, which can lead to increased control overhead and network convergence times. Another notable multicast routing protocol is the Distance Vector Multicast Routing Protocol (DVMRP), which is based on the Distance Vector algorithm and operates at the network layer to establish multicast distribution trees. DVMRP routers exchange routing updates to maintain multicast forwarding tables, enabling efficient delivery of multicast traffic to all group members. However,

DVMRP may not be as efficient as PIM or MOSPF in large-scale networks, as it relies on periodic updates and may suffer from slow convergence times and scalability issues in complex topologies. Additionally, DVMRP requires the maintenance of separate multicast routing tables, increasing management overhead and complexity. Source-Specific Multicast (SSM) is another multicast routing paradigm that simplifies the management of multicast traffic by restricting the source of multicast packets to a specific sender or set of senders. SSM eliminates the need for explicit join messages and multicast group membership tracking, as receivers explicitly specify the source of multicast traffic they wish to receive. This reduces control overhead and simplifies network configuration, making SSM particularly well-suited for content delivery and real-time streaming applications. However, SSM may not be suitable for applications that require multicast communication with multiple senders or dynamic group membership, as it restricts receivers to a single multicast source. Overall, multicast routing protocols are essential components of modern network architectures, enabling efficient distribution of data to multiple recipients and supporting a wide range of applications, including video streaming, online gaming, and content distribution networks. By understanding the capabilities and limitations of different multicast routing protocols, network administrators can design and deploy multicast-enabled networks that meet the specific requirements of their applications and users, ensuring optimal performance and scalability. Anycast deployment strategies are crucial for optimizing network performance and enhancing service availability by leveraging the concept of routing packets to the nearest or most optimal destination among multiple instances of the same service or resource distributed across different locations. The primary goal of anycast deployment is to route traffic to the nearest server or node in terms of network topology or latency, minimizing the time it takes for clients to connect to the desired service. Anycast achieves this by announcing the same IP address from multiple locations, allowing routers to select the best path based on metrics such as shortest AS path or lowest latency. One common use case for anycast deployment is in content delivery networks (CDNs), where multiple caching servers are distributed across various geographical locations to improve the delivery of web content, streaming media, or software downloads to end-users. By deploying anycast, CDNs can route user requests to the nearest caching server, reducing latency and improving the overall user experience. Another application of anycast deployment is in DNS infrastructure, where multiple authoritative name servers are distributed across different regions to enhance DNS resolution performance and mitigate the impact of DDoS attacks. Anycast DNS allows clients to connect to the nearest name server based on their geographic location or network proximity, reducing DNS resolution times and improving the reliability of DNS services. Deploying anycast for DNS resolution involves announcing the same set of IP addresses for authoritative name servers from multiple locations, allowing DNS queries to be routed to the nearest server based on network topology. This can be achieved using Border Gateway Protocol (BGP) routing announcements, where each anycast node advertises the same IP prefix with its own ASN to the global routing table. Network operators can use BGP attributes such as local preference, MED (Multi-Exit Discriminator), or AS path prepending to influence routing decisions and ensure traffic is directed to the desired anycast node. Anycast can also be deployed for load balancing and fault tolerance in distributed systems, such as global load balancers or service discovery mechanisms in cloud environments. By announcing the same IP address for load balancer instances deployed across multiple data centers or cloud regions, anycast allows clients to connect to the nearest load balancer node, distributing incoming requests evenly across the available backend servers and providing resilience against node failures or network outages. Deploying anycast for load balancing typically involves configuring BGP advertisements for the load balancer IP address and adjusting routing policies to achieve optimal traffic distribution and failover behavior. However, it's essential to carefully design anycast deployment strategies to avoid issues such as asymmetric routing, where traffic takes different paths to and from the anycast node, leading to suboptimal performance or routing loops. Network operators should also monitor the performance and health of anycast nodes using tools such as BGP monitoring or network telemetry to ensure proper functioning and troubleshoot any routing anomalies or service disruptions promptly. Additionally, anycast deployment may introduce challenges related to IP address management, network security, and operational complexity, requiring careful planning and coordination among stakeholders to address these concerns effectively. Overall, anycast deployment strategies play a critical role in optimizing network performance, enhancing service availability, and improving the scalability and resilience of distributed systems across various applications and use cases. By leveraging anycast routing techniques, organizations can deliver faster, more reliable, and highly available services to their users while minimizing operational overhead and infrastructure costs.

Chapter 4: Virtualization and Network Overlay Protocols

Network virtualization technologies have revolutionized the way we design, deploy, and manage networks, offering unprecedented flexibility, scalability, and efficiency in resource utilization. At its core, network virtualization decouples network services from the underlying hardware infrastructure, enabling the creation of virtualized network components, such as switches, routers, firewalls, and load balancers, that operate independently of physical devices. This abstraction layer allows multiple virtual networks to coexist on the same physical infrastructure, each with its own unique set of policies, configurations, and addressing schemes, providing isolation and security between different network tenants or applications. One of the key technologies driving network virtualization is software-defined networking (SDN), which separates the control plane from the data plane and centralizes network management and configuration in a software-based controller. With SDN, network administrators can dynamically provision and orchestrate network resources, automate configuration changes, and implement network-wide policies through programmable interfaces and APIs, such as OpenFlow. Deploying SDN typically involves installing an SDN controller, such as OpenDaylight or ONOS, and configuring network devices to communicate with the controller using the OpenFlow protocol. By abstracting network control from physical hardware, SDN simplifies network management, accelerates service delivery, and enables innovative network architectures, such as network slicing in 5G networks or micro-segmentation in cloud environments. Another key technology in network virtualization is network function virtualization (NFV), which virtualizes network services traditionally implemented in dedicated hardware appliances, such as firewalls, intrusion detection systems (IDS), or WAN accelerators, using standard virtualization techniques. NFV allows network services to be deployed as software-based virtual network functions (VNFs) on commodity hardware or cloud infrastructure, decoupling service delivery from specific hardware platforms and enabling greater agility and scalability in service deployment and scaling. To deploy NFV, organizations can use virtualization platforms, such as VMware vSphere or OpenStack, to instantiate VNFs as virtual machines or containers and deploy them on standard x86 servers or cloud instances. By virtualizing network functions, NFV reduces capital and operational expenses, accelerates service innovation, and enhances service agility and scalability, enabling operators to deliver new services more rapidly and cost-effectively. Additionally, network virtualization technologies enable the creation of virtual networks or overlay networks that run on top of physical infrastructure, providing logical isolation, segmentation, and customization of network resources for different applications or user groups. Overlay networks, such as virtual extensible LANs (VXLAN) or generic routing encapsulation (GRE), encapsulate traffic from virtual machines or containers and tunnel it over the underlying physical network, allowing multiple virtual networks to share the same physical infrastructure without interfering with each other. Deploying overlay networks involves configuring tunnel endpoints on network devices, such as switches or routers, and configuring virtual network identifiers (VNIs) or tunneling protocols to distinguish between different overlay networks. By virtualizing network resources, overlay networks provide greater flexibility, scalability, and efficiency in network design and operation, enabling organizations to support diverse application requirements and scale network capacity as needed. In summary, network virtualization technologies play a crucial role in modernizing and transforming traditional networking architectures, offering unprecedented flexibility, scalability, and agility in deploying and managing network resources. By decoupling network services from underlying hardware, SDN, NFV, and overlay technologies empower organizations to build more agile, efficient, and scalable networks that can adapt to changing business requirements and support emerging applications and services in an increasingly digital and interconnected world. Overlay protocols for virtual networks play a pivotal role in modern network architectures, enabling the creation of virtualized network overlays that run on top of physical infrastructure, providing logical isolation, segmentation, and customization of network resources for different applications or user groups. One of the prominent overlay protocols widely used in virtual networking is Virtual Extensible LAN (VXLAN), which is designed to address the scalability limitations of traditional VLANs by allowing the creation of up to 16 million virtual networks or segments, known as VXLAN segments or VXLAN segments, each with its own unique 24-bit VXLAN network identifier (VNI). VXLAN encapsulates Layer 2 Ethernet frames within UDP packets, enabling them to be transmitted across Layer 3 IP networks, thereby extending Layer 2 connectivity beyond the boundaries of a single Layer 2 domain. Deploying VXLAN involves configuring VXLAN tunnel endpoints (VTEPs) on network devices, such as switches or routers, and mapping VLANs or virtual ports to VXLAN segments to establish connectivity between virtual and physical networks. Another widely used overlay protocol is Generic Routing Encapsulation (GRE), which encapsulates Layer 3 IP packets within IP packets, providing a simple and flexible mechanism for creating overlay networks over IP networks. GRE tunnels establish point-to-point connections between tunnel endpoints, allowing packets to be encapsulated and transmitted across the underlying IP network without modification. To deploy GRE tunnels, network administrators configure tunnel interfaces on routers or switches and define the source and destination IP addresses of the tunnel endpoints, along with any relevant tunnel parameters, such as tunnel key or tunnel mode. Additionally, Network Virtualization using Generic Routing Encapsulation (NVGRE) is another overlay protocol that provides similar functionality to VXLAN and GRE by encapsulating Layer 2 Ethernet frames within IP packets, allowing them to be transmitted across IP networks. NVGRE uses a 24-bit Tenant Network Identifier (TNI) to distinguish between different virtual networks and facilitate segmentation and isolation of network traffic. Deploying NVGRE involves configuring NVGRE tunnel endpoints (NVEs) on network devices and defining mappings between virtual ports or VLANs and NVGRE tunnels to establish connectivity between virtual and physical networks. Furthermore, Stateless Transport Tunneling (STT) is a lightweight overlay protocol developed by Nicira (now part of VMware) that encapsulates Layer 2 Ethernet frames within UDP packets, providing a simple and efficient mechanism for creating overlay networks in virtualized environments. STT tunnels establish point-to-point connections between tunnel endpoints, allowing packets to be encapsulated and transmitted across the underlying IP network without modification. Deploying STT involves configuring STT tunnel endpoints on network devices and defining mappings between virtual ports or VLANs and STT tunnels to establish connectivity between virtual and physical networks. Overall, overlay protocols for virtual networks enable organizations to create flexible, scalable, and efficient network architectures that can adapt to changing business requirements and support diverse application workloads. Whether it's VXLAN, GRE, NVGRE, or STT, each overlay protocol offers unique features and capabilities to meet the needs of specific use cases and deployment scenarios, empowering organizations to build robust and resilient network infrastructures that can deliver superior performance, security, and agility in today's dynamic and evolving IT environments.

Chapter 5: Software-Defined Networking (SDN) Protocols

Software-Defined Networking (SDN) architecture and its components represent a paradigm shift in the way networks are designed, deployed, and managed, offering unprecedented flexibility, scalability, and automation to meet the demands of modern IT environments. At the core of SDN architecture is the decoupling of the control plane from the data plane, enabling centralized control and programmability of network devices through a software-based controller. One of the key components of SDN architecture is the SDN controller, which serves as the centralized brain of the network, responsible for making forwarding decisions and enforcing network policies based on high-level instructions received from the SDN application layer or network administrator. Popular SDN controllers include OpenDaylight, ONOS, and Ryu, each offering unique features and capabilities to support diverse use cases and deployment scenarios. To deploy an SDN controller, network administrators typically download the controller software package from the official website or repository and install it on a dedicated server or virtual machine using standard installation commands or scripts. Once the SDN controller is up and running, administrators can use its management interface, often accessible via a web-based dashboard or command-line interface, to configure network policies, define forwarding rules, and monitor network traffic in real-time. Another critical component of SDN architecture is the southbound interface, which serves as the communication link between the SDN controller and network devices, enabling the controller to interact with switches, routers, and other network elements to program their forwarding behavior and collect network statistics. Common southbound interfaces include OpenFlow, NETCONF, and RESTCONF, each offering different levels of programmability and functionality to support diverse network environments. To configure a southbound interface on a network device, administrators typically enable the respective protocol or API on the device and configure the necessary parameters, such as controller IP address, port number, and authentication credentials, using configuration commands or management interfaces provided by the device vendor. Additionally, SDN architecture includes the northbound interface, which allows SDN applications or orchestration systems to communicate with the SDN controller, enabling the development and deployment of custom network services, applications, and automation workflows. Northbound interfaces typically expose RESTful APIs or SDKs that developers can use to interact with the SDN controller and integrate it with other IT systems and services. To develop an SDN application, developers typically use programming languages such as Python, Java, or Go and leverage SDKs or libraries provided by the SDN controller vendor to access controller functions and services programmatically. Furthermore, SDN architecture often includes network virtualization technologies, such as Virtual Extensible LAN (VXLAN) or Network Virtualization using Generic Routing Encapsulation (NVGRE), which enable the creation of virtual networks or segments that are logically isolated from each other, providing enhanced security, scalability, and flexibility. To deploy network virtualization in an SDN environment, administrators typically configure virtual network overlays on the SDN controller using network management tools or APIs provided by the controller vendor. In summary, SDN architecture and its components represent a fundamental shift in the way networks are designed, deployed, and managed, offering unprecedented levels of agility, scalability, and automation to meet the evolving demands of modern IT environments. By decoupling the control plane from the data plane and centralizing network intelligence in software-based controllers, SDN enables organizations to create dynamic, programmable, and adaptive network infrastructures that can support diverse applications, services, and workloads with ease. SDN protocols for network control play a crucial role in enabling the programmability and automation of network infrastructure, facilitating dynamic provisioning, policy enforcement, and traffic engineering in software-defined environments. One of the most widely adopted SDN protocols is OpenFlow, which defines a standard communication interface between the SDN controller and forwarding devices, allowing the controller to manage packet forwarding behavior and traffic flows in the network. To deploy OpenFlow in an SDN environment, network administrators typically configure OpenFlow-enabled switches or routers to establish a connection with the SDN controller and exchange flow table entries and control messages using the OpenFlow protocol. Another prominent SDN protocol is NETCONF (Network Configuration Protocol), which provides a standardized mechanism for configuring and managing network devices, including routers, switches, and firewalls, over a secure transport layer. To deploy NETCONF in an SDN environment, administrators typically enable the NETCONF server on network devices and configure access control policies to restrict access to authorized users or applications. Additionally,

RESTCONF (RESTful Network Configuration Protocol) is gaining traction as a lightweight, web-based alternative to NETCONF, allowing network administrators to perform configuration and management tasks using HTTP methods such as GET, POST, PUT, and DELETE. To deploy RESTCONF in an SDN environment, administrators typically enable the RESTCONF service on the SDN controller and configure access control policies to secure API endpoints and enforce authentication and authorization requirements. Moreover, gRPC (gRPC Remote Procedure Calls) is emerging as a promising SDN protocol for high-performance, bidirectional communication between the SDN controller and network devices, enabling efficient data exchange and control plane interactions over a secure and efficient transport layer. To deploy gRPC in an SDN environment, administrators typically enable gRPC support on the SDN controller and configure client-server connections using gRPC APIs and libraries provided by the controller vendor. Furthermore, BGP-LS (Border Gateway Protocol-Link State) is gaining attention as a scalable and extensible protocol for distributing network topology and traffic engineering information between the SDN controller and edge routers, enabling real-time visibility and control of network resources and paths. To deploy BGP-LS in an SDN environment, administrators typically configure BGP-LS sessions between the SDN controller and edge routers and exchange link state information using BGP-LS messages and attributes. Additionally, PCEP (Path Computation Element Protocol) is a specialized SDN protocol for dynamic path computation and provisioning in traffic-engineered networks, allowing the SDN controller to request path computation services from external Path Computation Elements (PCEs) and program forwarding devices with optimal traffic paths. To deploy PCEP in an SDN environment, administrators typically configure PCEP sessions between the SDN controller and PCEs and exchange path computation requests and responses using PCEP messages and attributes. In summary, SDN protocols for network control play a critical role in enabling the programmability, automation, and orchestration of network infrastructure, allowing organizations to create agile, flexible, and efficient network environments that can adapt to changing business requirements and application demands.

Chapter 6: Peer-to-Peer Networking Protocols

Peer discovery and communication protocols are fundamental components of distributed systems, enabling nodes to identify and communicate with each other in a network environment. One widely used peer discovery protocol is the Domain Name System (DNS), which translates domain names into IP addresses and vice versa, facilitating the resolution of hostnames to IP addresses and enabling communication between devices on the Internet. To deploy DNS in a network, administrators typically configure DNS servers to store and manage domain name records, such as A records (IPv4 addresses) and AAAA records (IPv6 addresses), and configure client devices to use DNS servers for hostname resolution using the nslookup or dig command-line utilities. Another essential peer discovery protocol is the Dynamic Host Configuration Protocol (DHCP), which automates the assignment of IP addresses, subnet masks, and other network configuration parameters to client devices on a network, simplifying network administration and reducing configuration errors. To deploy DHCP in a network, administrators typically configure DHCP servers to allocate IP addresses from a predefined pool and lease duration and configure DHCP clients to obtain network configuration settings dynamically using the dhclient or ipconfig command-line utilities. Additionally, the Simple Network Management Protocol (SNMP) is commonly used for peer discovery and communication in network management systems, allowing administrators to monitor and manage network devices, such as routers, switches, and servers, using a standardized set of management information and protocols. To deploy SNMP in a network, administrators typically enable SNMP agents on network devices and configure SNMP managers to collect and process SNMP traps and queries using SNMP management tools or libraries. Moreover, the Bonjour protocol, also known as Zeroconf or mDNS (Multicast DNS), enables peer discovery and communication in local networks without the need for centralized servers or configuration, allowing devices to discover and communicate with each other using multicast DNS queries and responses. To deploy Bonjour in a network, administrators typically enable mDNS support on compatible devices and configure network settings to allow multicast traffic using the avahi-daemon or mdns-repeater command-line utilities. Furthermore, the Link Layer Discovery Protocol (LLDP) is a vendor-neutral protocol that enables devices to advertise their capabilities and network connectivity information to neighboring devices, facilitating automatic neighbor discovery and topology mapping in Ethernet networks. To deploy LLDP in a network, administrators typically enable LLDP support on network devices and configure LLDP settings to advertise system information and network interfaces using the lldpctl or lldpcli command-line utilities. Additionally, the Service Location Protocol (SLP) is a standards-based protocol that enables devices and services to advertise their presence and capabilities on a network, allowing clients to discover and access available services dynamically. To deploy SLP in a network, administrators typically enable SLP agents on devices and configure service registrations and queries using SLP management tools or libraries. In summary, peer discovery and communication protocols are essential building blocks of modern networks, enabling devices to discover and communicate with each other seamlessly, facilitating the automation, management, and scalability of network infrastructure.

P2P (Peer-to-Peer) network management and security are crucial aspects of modern network infrastructures, especially in decentralized environments where devices communicate directly with each other without the need for centralized servers or intermediaries. P2P networks rely on a distributed architecture where each node in the network can act as both a client and a server, sharing resources and information with other nodes. Managing and securing P2P networks pose unique challenges due to their decentralized nature and the potential for unauthorized access and malicious activities. One common approach to managing P2P networks is through the use of P2P management protocols, such as the BitTorrent Protocol, which facilitates the distribution and sharing of files among peers in a decentralized manner. To deploy the BitTorrent Protocol, users typically use BitTorrent clients, such as µTorrent or qBittorrent, to connect to the BitTorrent network and download or share files using torrent files or magnet links. However, managing security in P2P networks requires additional measures to protect against potential threats, such as unauthorized access, data breaches, and malware propagation. One key security concern in P2P networks is data integrity, as files shared among peers may be susceptible to tampering or modification by malicious actors. To address this concern, users can employ cryptographic techniques, such as digital signatures and hash functions, to verify the authenticity and integrity of files downloaded from P2P networks. Additionally, encryption can be used to protect communication between peers in P2P networks, preventing eavesdropping and data interception by unauthorized parties. Another security measure for P2P networks is access control, where users can implement authentication mechanisms to restrict access to shared resources and ensure that only authorized peers can participate in file sharing and communication. This can be achieved through the use of access control lists (ACLs) or user authentication protocols, such as OAuth or OpenID. Furthermore, network segmentation can help improve security in P2P networks by isolating different groups of peers and limiting the scope of potential security breaches. By dividing the network into smaller segments and applying access controls and security policies to each segment, administrators can reduce the attack surface and mitigate the impact of security incidents. Additionally, intrusion detection and prevention systems (IDPS) can be deployed in P2P networks to monitor network traffic and detect suspicious activities or unauthorized access attempts in real-time. IDPS solutions can analyze network packets, log files, and system events to identify potential security threats and take proactive measures to prevent or mitigate them. Moreover, regular security audits and vulnerability assessments are essential for identifying and addressing security weaknesses in P2P networks. By conducting periodic audits and assessments, administrators can evaluate the effectiveness of existing security measures, identify potential vulnerabilities, and implement necessary patches and updates to strengthen security posture. In summary, P2P network management and security are critical considerations for ensuring the integrity, availability, and confidentiality of shared resources and communication in decentralized network environments. By implementing robust management and security measures, organizations can effectively manage and protect their P2P networks against potential threats and vulnerabilities.

Chapter 7: Internet of Things (IoT) Protocols and Integration

IoT (Internet of Things) communication protocols play a crucial role in facilitating communication between IoT devices and enabling the exchange of data and commands in IoT ecosystems. These protocols define the rules and conventions for how devices communicate with each other and with central systems, allowing for seamless interoperability and integration across diverse IoT environments. One of the most widely used IoT communication protocols is MQTT (Message Queuing Telemetry Transport), which is a lightweight and efficient publish-subscribe messaging protocol designed for low-bandwidth, high-latency networks. MQTT operates on top of the TCP/IP protocol stack and is commonly used in IoT applications for its simplicity, reliability, and scalability. To deploy MQTT in an IoT system, users typically need to set up an MQTT broker, which acts as a centralized messaging hub that facilitates communication between IoT devices. Popular MQTT brokers include Mosquitto, Eclipse Paho, and HiveMQ, which can be installed and configured using CLI commands or through graphical user interfaces (GUIs). Once the MQTT broker is set up,

IoT devices can connect to the broker using MQTT client libraries and publish or subscribe to topics to exchange messages with other devices or applications. Another commonly used IoT communication protocol is CoAP (Constrained Application Protocol), which is designed for resource-constrained devices and networks, such as those found in IoT deployments. CoAP is based on the REST architectural style and operates over UDP or DTLS (Datagram Transport Layer Security), making it lightweight and suitable for constrained environments. To deploy CoAP in an IoT system, users can utilize CoAP client and server implementations, such as Californium or libcoap, which provide APIs for interacting with CoAP resources and handling CoAP messages. CoAP can be used for various IoT use cases, including sensor data collection, device control, and firmware updates, thanks to its support for request-response interactions and asynchronous notifications. Additionally, HTTP (Hypertext Transfer Protocol) is commonly used as an IoT communication protocol, especially for web-based IoT applications and integrations with existing web services and APIs. HTTP provides a familiar and standardized interface for accessing IoT resources and exchanging data over the internet, making it suitable for a wide range of IoT use cases. To deploy HTTP in an IoT system, users can leverage HTTP client and server libraries, such as cURL or Node.js, to send and receive HTTP requests and responses between IoT devices and servers. Furthermore, WebSockets is emerging as a popular IoT communication protocol for real-time, bidirectional communication between devices and web applications. WebSockets enable persistent, low-latency connections between clients and servers, allowing for efficient data streaming and interactive communication in IoT deployments. To deploy WebSockets in an IoT system, users can utilize WebSocket client and server libraries, such as Socket.IO or Autobahn, which provide APIs for establishing WebSocket connections and exchanging messages in real-time. In summary, IoT communication protocols play a vital role in enabling communication between IoT devices and facilitating the exchange of data and commands in IoT ecosystems. By leveraging protocols such as MQTT, CoAP, HTTP, and WebSockets, organizations can build scalable, interoperable, and secure IoT solutions that meet the diverse needs of modern IoT applications.

IoT device integration strategies are essential for effectively incorporating IoT devices into existing infrastructure and systems, ensuring seamless communication, interoperability, and data exchange. One common strategy for integrating IoT devices is through the use of IoT platforms, which provide a centralized framework for managing and connecting devices, collecting and analyzing data, and orchestrating workflows. Platforms such as AWS IoT, Microsoft Azure IoT, and Google Cloud IoT offer a range of services and tools for device management, data ingestion, analytics, and application development, making it easier for organizations to deploy and scale IoT solutions. To integrate IoT devices with these platforms, users typically need to register their devices, provision security credentials, and configure device communication settings using platform-specific APIs or CLI commands. Another integration strategy involves using IoT middleware, which acts as an intermediary layer between IoT devices and applications, providing services such as protocol translation, data transformation, and event processing. Middleware solutions like MQTT brokers, CoAP proxies, and edge computing platforms enable seamless integration of heterogeneous devices and protocols, allowing for efficient data exchange and communication in IoT deployments. To deploy IoT middleware, users can install and configure middleware components on edge devices, gateways, or cloud servers using platform-specific installation guides or deployment scripts. Additionally, organizations can leverage existing enterprise integration platforms, such as Apache Kafka, RabbitMQ, or Apache NiFi, to integrate IoT data streams with enterprise systems and applications. These platforms offer robust messaging and streaming capabilities, along with connectors and adapters for integrating IoT data with databases, analytics tools, and business applications. To integrate IoT data with enterprise systems using Kafka, for example, users can configure Kafka Connect connectors to ingest data from IoT devices into Kafka topics and then use Kafka Streams or KSQL for real-time data processing and analysis. Furthermore, organizations can implement custom integration solutions using APIs, SDKs, and development frameworks to build bespoke IoT integrations tailored to their specific requirements and use cases. By developing custom integrations, organizations can leverage their existing infrastructure, expertise, and technology stack to seamlessly integrate IoT devices with backend systems, applications, and processes. To develop custom integrations, developers can use programming languages such as Python, Java, or Node.js to create APIs, microservices, or event-driven workflows that handle device communication, data processing, and integration logic. Additionally, organizations can adopt standard IoT communication protocols and data formats, such as MQTT, JSON, or OPC UA, to ensure compatibility and interoperability with existing systems and industry standards. In summary, IoT device integration strategies are critical for enabling seamless communication, interoperability, and data exchange in IoT deployments. By leveraging IoT platforms, middleware, enterprise integration platforms, and custom integration solutions, organizations can effectively integrate IoT devices with existing infrastructure and systems, enabling them to unlock the full potential of IoT technology and drive business value.

Chapter 8: Content Delivery Network (CDN) Protocols

CDN architecture and functionality play a crucial role in optimizing content delivery and enhancing the performance and reliability of web applications and services. A Content Delivery Network (CDN) is a distributed network of servers strategically deployed across various geographic locations to efficiently deliver content to end-users. CDN architecture typically consists of multiple layers, including edge servers, caching servers, and origin servers, working together to accelerate content delivery and improve user experience. Edge servers are the front-line servers in the CDN architecture, located close to end-users in different regions or cities. These servers cache and serve static and dynamic content, such as images, videos, scripts, and web pages, to users requesting them. Edge servers are responsible for minimizing latency and reducing the load on origin servers by serving content from the nearest edge location. To deploy edge servers in a CDN architecture, organizations can use CDN providers' management consoles or APIs to provision and configure edge server instances in specific geographic regions. Providers like Cloudflare, Akamai, and Amazon CloudFront offer user-friendly interfaces and APIs for managing CDN resources and configuring edge server settings. Caching servers are another essential component of CDN architecture, responsible for storing and serving cached copies of content to users. These servers cache frequently accessed content at the edge locations, reducing the need to fetch content from origin servers repeatedly. By caching content closer to end-users, caching servers improve response times and reduce network congestion, resulting in faster and more reliable content delivery. Organizations can configure caching settings and cache expiration policies using CDN provider consoles or APIs to control how content is cached and served to users. Origin servers form the backend infrastructure of the CDN architecture, hosting the original source content and acting as the authoritative source for content delivery. When a request for content is not available in the cache or has expired, edge servers retrieve the content from origin servers and cache it for future requests. Organizations can deploy origin servers in their data centers or on cloud platforms like AWS, Azure, or Google Cloud Platform (GCP), depending on their requirements and infrastructure setup. CDN providers offer integrations with origin servers, allowing organizations to configure origin settings, such as caching rules, security policies, and access controls, through their management interfaces or APIs. Additionally, CDN architectures may include other components such as load balancers, security features, and analytics tools to further enhance performance, security, and insights into content delivery. Load balancers distribute incoming traffic across multiple edge servers, ensuring optimal resource utilization and availability. Security features, such as DDoS protection, web application firewall (WAF), and SSL/TLS encryption, safeguard content and infrastructure from malicious attacks and unauthorized access. Analytics tools provide insights into CDN performance, user behavior, and content consumption patterns, enabling organizations to optimize content delivery strategies and improve user experience. To configure load balancers, security features, and analytics tools in a CDN architecture, organizations can use provider-specific management consoles or APIs to customize settings and monitor performance metrics. In summary, CDN architecture and functionality are essential for optimizing content delivery, enhancing performance, and ensuring the reliability and security of web applications and services. By leveraging edge servers, caching servers, origin servers, and other components, organizations can deliver content efficiently to users worldwide, improving user experience and achieving business objectives.

CDN optimization protocols are crucial for enhancing the performance, reliability, and efficiency of Content Delivery Networks (CDNs) by implementing various techniques and algorithms to optimize content delivery. One of the fundamental protocols used in CDN optimization is the HTTP protocol, which governs the communication between web servers and clients, including browsers and mobile devices. By optimizing HTTP interactions, CDNs can minimize latency, reduce bandwidth consumption, and accelerate content delivery to end-users. One common optimization technique is HTTP/2, an enhanced version of the HTTP protocol that introduces features like multiplexing, header compression, and server push to improve performance and efficiency. To deploy HTTP/2 in a CDN environment, administrators can enable support for the protocol on edge servers and origin servers using configuration settings or command-line options. For example, in Nginx, a popular web server software, administrators can enable HTTP/2 support by adding the "http2" directive to the server block configuration file. Another important CDN optimization protocol is TLS (Transport Layer Security), which provides secure communication between clients and servers by encrypting data transmitted over the network. By deploying TLS encryption, CDNs can protect sensitive information, such as user credentials, payment details, and personal data, from unauthorized access and eavesdropping attacks. To enable TLS encryption in a CDN environment, administrators can obtain SSL/TLS certificates from trusted certificate authorities (CAs) and configure edge servers to use HTTPS (HTTP over TLS) for secure communication with clients. Command-line tools like OpenSSL can be used to generate SSL/TLS certificate signing requests (CSRs), obtain certificates from CAs, and configure SSL/TLS settings on web servers. Additionally, CDNs can optimize content delivery by implementing caching mechanisms and content compression techniques. Caching enables CDNs to store copies of frequently accessed content at edge locations, reducing the need to fetch content from origin servers repeatedly. By caching content closer to end-users, CDNs can improve response times, minimize latency, and decrease bandwidth consumption. Content compression techniques, such as GZIP compression, further enhance performance by reducing the size of web pages, images, and other resources transmitted over the network. Administrators can configure caching settings and content compression options on edge servers to optimize content delivery in a CDN environment. For example, in Apache HTTP Server, administrators can enable GZIP compression by adding directives to the server configuration file and specify caching rules using directives like "Cache-Control" and "Expires". Additionally, CDNs can optimize content delivery by implementing traffic management techniques, such as load balancing and traffic shaping, to distribute incoming requests evenly across multiple edge servers and prioritize critical traffic based on predefined policies. Load balancing algorithms like round-robin, least connections, and weighted round-robin can be used to distribute traffic effectively and improve scalability, fault tolerance, and availability in CDN environments. To deploy load balancing in a CDN architecture, administrators can use command-line tools like HAProxy or Nginx to configure load balancers and define load balancing algorithms and health checks. Overall, CDN optimization protocols play a critical role in improving the performance, reliability, and security of Content Delivery Networks by implementing various techniques and algorithms to optimize content delivery, secure communication, and manage traffic effectively. By deploying protocols like HTTP/2, TLS, caching, content compression, and traffic management, CDNs can enhance user experience, reduce latency, and achieve better overall performance for web applications and services.

Chapter 9: Next-Generation Protocol Developments

Protocols for future network technologies play a pivotal role in shaping the landscape of communication, connectivity, and data exchange in the ever-evolving digital world. As we venture into the realm of futuristic technologies such as 5G, Internet of Things (IoT), artificial intelligence (AI), and edge computing, the need for robust, efficient, and scalable protocols becomes increasingly evident. One of the most anticipated protocols for future networks is IPv6 (Internet Protocol version 6), designed to address the limitations of IPv4 and accommodate the growing number of connected devices. IPv6 offers a significantly larger address space, improved security features, and enhanced support for mobility and autoconfiguration. Deploying IPv6 involves configuring network devices, such as routers, switches, and firewalls, to support the protocol and enable IPv6 connectivity. Command-line tools like Cisco IOS commands can be used to configure IPv6 addressing, routing, and access control lists (ACLs) on Cisco routers and switches. Another critical protocol for future network technologies is QUIC (Quick UDP Internet Connections), a transport protocol developed by

Google to optimize web traffic and improve user experience. QUIC combines the features of TCP and UDP while adding additional functionalities like connection multiplexing, stream encryption, and forward error correction (FEC). Deploying QUIC requires enabling support for the protocol on web servers and clients and configuring firewall rules to allow QUIC traffic. In NGINX, administrators can enable QUIC support by compiling NGINX with the ngx_quic module and configuring QUIC parameters in the server block configuration file. Additionally, protocols like HTTP/3, based on QUIC, are expected to revolutionize web communication by offering faster, more reliable connections and reducing latency and packet loss. HTTP/3 deployment involves enabling support for the protocol on web servers and clients and configuring settings like server push, header compression, and prioritization. Tools like curl commands can be used to test HTTP/3 connectivity and performance by sending requests to HTTP/3-enabled servers and analyzing response times and error codes. As the demand for high-speed, low-latency communication grows, protocols like Multi-Access Edge Computing (MEC) and Network Function Virtualization (NFV) are gaining prominence. MEC allows applications to run closer to end-users at the edge of the network, reducing latency and improving performance. NFV enables virtualization of network functions, such as firewalls, load balancers, and intrusion detection systems, making it easier to deploy, scale, and manage network services. Deploying MEC and NFV involves deploying virtualized infrastructure, orchestrating virtual network functions (VNFs), and configuring service chains to route traffic through virtualized network services. Tools like OpenStack and Kubernetes can be used to deploy and manage virtualized infrastructure and applications in MEC and NFV environments. Additionally, emerging protocols like Named Data Networking (NDN) and Information-Centric Networking (ICN) are redefining how data is accessed, stored, and distributed on the internet. NDN replaces traditional IP-based communication with named data objects, enabling content-based routing and caching at the network layer. ICN focuses on content-centric communication, where data is addressed by its content rather than its location, leading to more efficient data delivery and reduced reliance on centralized servers. Deploying NDN and ICN involves implementing new network architectures, protocols, and applications that support content-based communication and caching. Tools like CCNx and NDN Forwarder can be used to deploy NDN routers and test NDN-based applications in experimental network environments. In summary, protocols for future network technologies are essential for driving innovation, enabling new services, and addressing the challenges of an increasingly connected and data-driven world. By embracing protocols like IPv6, QUIC, HTTP/3, MEC, NFV, NDN, and ICN, organizations can build scalable, efficient, and resilient network infrastructures that meet the demands of tomorrow's digital landscape.

Innovations in protocol design have been instrumental in shaping the evolution of communication networks, driving efficiency, scalability, and security across various technological domains. One notable innovation in protocol design is the development of IPv6, which addresses the limitations of its predecessor, IPv4, by providing a significantly larger address space, enhanced security features, and support for emerging technologies such as Internet of Things (IoT) and 5G networks. Deploying IPv6 involves configuring network devices to support the protocol, enabling IPv6 addressing, and ensuring compatibility with existing IPv4 infrastructure through techniques like dual-stack configuration. Another significant innovation is the emergence of QUIC (Quick UDP Internet Connections), a transport protocol developed by Google to optimize web traffic and improve user experience. QUIC combines the features of TCP and UDP while adding features like connection multiplexing, stream encryption, and forward error correction (FEC), making it well-suited for applications requiring low-latency and high-throughput communication. Deploying QUIC involves enabling support for the protocol on web servers and clients, configuring firewall rules to allow QUIC traffic, and optimizing QUIC parameters for specific use cases. Additionally, HTTP/3, based on QUIC, represents a significant advancement in web communication protocols, offering faster, more reliable connections and reducing latency and packet loss compared to its predecessors. Deploying HTTP/3 requires enabling support for the protocol on web servers and clients, configuring settings like server push and header compression, and testing compatibility with existing web applications and infrastructure. Another innovation in protocol design is the development of Multi-Access Edge Computing (MEC) protocols, which enable applications to run closer to end-users at the edge of the network, reducing latency and improving performance. MEC protocols leverage technologies like network slicing, edge caching, and service chaining to provide low-latency access to computing resources and data processing capabilities at the network edge. Deploying MEC involves deploying virtualized infrastructure, orchestrating edge applications, and configuring network policies to optimize resource utilization and ensure quality of service (QoS) for edge services. Additionally, innovations in protocol design have led to the development of Information-Centric Networking (ICN) and Named Data Networking (NDN) protocols, which prioritize content-based communication and caching over traditional IP-based routing. ICN and NDN protocols enable efficient content delivery, reduce reliance on centralized servers, and improve scalability and resilience in distributed communication environments. Deploying ICN and NDN involves implementing new network architectures, protocols, and applications that support content-based communication and caching, as well as testing and optimizing ICN/NDN deployments for specific use cases and network topologies. Overall, innovations in protocol design continue to drive advancements in communication networks, enabling new services, improving performance, and addressing the evolving needs of modern digital environments.

Chapter 10: Emerging Trends and Future Directions in Network Communication

Trends shaping the future of networking are dynamic and multifaceted, reflecting the rapid evolution of technology and the ever-changing needs of businesses and consumers in today's digital landscape. One prominent trend is the rise of Software-Defined Networking (SDN), which decouples network control from hardware and enables centralized management and programmability of network resources through software-based controllers. Deploying SDN involves configuring SDN controllers, such as OpenDaylight or ONOS, using commands like "sudo ovs-vsctl set-controller" to define the control plane and orchestrate network policies. Additionally, Network Functions Virtualization (NFV) is gaining traction as organizations seek to virtualize network services and functions to improve agility, scalability, and cost-effectiveness. NFV allows network services, such as firewalls, load balancers, and routers, to run as software instances on commodity hardware, reducing the need for dedicated appliances and streamlining network management. Deploying NFV involves deploying virtualized network functions (VNFs) using orchestration tools like OpenStack or Kubernetes, with commands like "kubectl create -f" to deploy VNF pods and "kubectl scale" to adjust resource allocation dynamically. Another trend is the proliferation of cloud-native networking, driven by the adoption of cloud computing and containerization technologies like Docker and Kubernetes. Cloud-native networking architectures leverage microservices, container orchestration, and cloud-native networking solutions like Istio and Linkerd to provide scalable, resilient, and secure communication between cloud-based applications and services. Deploying cloud-native networking involves configuring service meshes, defining routing rules, and managing traffic policies using command-line tools like "istioctl" or "kubectl." Moreover, the Internet of Things (IoT) continues to reshape networking paradigms, as billions of connected devices generate vast amounts of data and require seamless connectivity and communication. IoT networking technologies, such as Low-Power Wide-Area Networks (LPWANs), Bluetooth Low Energy (BLE), and Zigbee, enable efficient and reliable communication between IoT devices and gateways, facilitating the deployment of smart city, industrial automation, and healthcare applications. Deploying IoT networks involves provisioning IoT devices, configuring network protocols and gateways, and implementing security measures to protect sensitive data and devices from cyber threats. Furthermore, the integration of Artificial Intelligence (AI) and Machine Learning (ML) into networking infrastructure is poised to revolutionize network management, optimization, and security. AI-driven network analytics platforms leverage ML algorithms to analyze network traffic patterns, predict performance issues, and automate remediation actions, enhancing network visibility, and operational efficiency. Deploying AI-driven network analytics involves collecting telemetry data from network devices, training ML models using frameworks like TensorFlow or PyTorch, and deploying inference engines to make real-time decisions based on network insights. Additionally, the convergence of networking and edge computing is shaping the future of distributed computing architectures, enabling latency-sensitive applications to run closer to end-users and devices at the network edge. Edge networking technologies, such as Mobile Edge Computing (MEC) and Edge Cloud, leverage edge resources to process data locally, reducing latency and bandwidth usage and improving application performance. Deploying edge networking involves deploying edge computing infrastructure, optimizing workload placement, and implementing edge caching and content delivery mechanisms to enhance user experience. In summary, the future of networking is characterized by agility, automation, and intelligence, driven by trends like SDN, NFV, cloud-native networking, IoT, AI, ML, and edge computing. As organizations embrace digital transformation and embrace these trends, they will be better positioned to meet the evolving demands of modern applications, users, and business requirements.

Predictions for network communication evolution indicate a transformative journey driven by emerging technologies, evolving user behaviors, and shifting industry landscapes. One of the key predictions is the widespread adoption of 5G technology, which promises to revolutionize network communication by delivering faster data speeds, lower latency, and greater network capacity. With commands like "sudo nmcli c up" for activating network connections or "iwconfig" for configuring wireless network interfaces, 5G networks are poised to enable innovative applications and services such as augmented reality, autonomous vehicles, and remote healthcare. Moreover, the Internet of Things (IoT) is expected to continue its exponential growth, leading to a proliferation of connected devices and sensors that communicate and exchange data over networks. IoT devices leverage protocols like MQTT or CoAP for efficient communication, enabling smart homes, smart cities, and industrial automation. Additionally, Artificial Intelligence (AI) and Machine Learning (ML) are anticipated to play a significant role in network communication evolution, enabling intelligent network management, predictive analytics, and automated security threat detection and response. ML algorithms analyze network traffic patterns and anomalies to identify potential security threats, while AI-driven network optimization techniques enhance performance and reliability. Furthermore, the convergence of networking and edge computing is expected to reshape network architectures, enabling data processing and analytics to occur closer to the source of data generation. Edge computing technologies like Kubernetes or Docker Swarm facilitate the deployment of containerized applications and services at the network edge, reducing latency and improving scalability. Another prediction is the rise of blockchain technology in network communication, offering enhanced security, transparency, and decentralized control over data transactions. Blockchain-based networks use commands like "geth" for interacting with Ethereum networks or "bitcoin-cli" for managing Bitcoin transactions, providing a secure and tamper-proof ledger for recording and verifying network activities. Moreover, Quantum Computing is anticipated to have a transformative impact on network communication, enabling faster cryptographic algorithms, enhanced encryption techniques, and more efficient data processing. Quantum networks leverage quantum entanglement and superposition to transmit information securely over long distances, offering unparalleled levels of security and reliability. Additionally, advancements in network virtualization and Software-Defined Networking (SDN) are expected to continue, enabling organizations to dynamically allocate and manage network resources based on application requirements. SDN controllers like Ryu or Floodlight provide centralized control and programmability of network infrastructure, facilitating automation and orchestration of network services. In summary, the future of network communication is characterized by rapid innovation, driven by emerging technologies, changing user needs, and evolving industry trends. By embracing these predictions and leveraging the power of advanced networking technologies, organizations can unlock new opportunities, drive digital transformation, and deliver enhanced user experiences in the increasingly connected world.

Conclusion

In summary, "Network Engineer's Bible: Mastering 100 Protocols for Communication, Management, and Security" offers a comprehensive and in-depth exploration of networking protocols across four essential books. In "Foundations of Networking," beginners are provided with a solid understanding of fundamental protocols, laying the groundwork for their journey into the world of networking. "Navigating Network Management" equips network engineers with the knowledge and skills to efficiently operate networks by mastering a range of protocols tailored for management tasks. "Securing the Network" delves into the protocols, practices, and strategies necessary for safeguarding data and protecting networks from cyber threats, ensuring the integrity and confidentiality of critical information. Finally, "Advanced Protocol Dynamics" delves into complex network communication strategies, providing experienced engineers with the tools and insights needed to tackle intricate networking challenges. Together, these four books serve as an indispensable resource for network engineers at all levels, empowering them to navigate the ever-evolving landscape of network communication, management, and security with confidence and expertise. Whether you are a beginner looking to establish a solid foundation or an experienced professional seeking to enhance your skills, "Network Engineer's Bible" offers a comprehensive guide to mastering the intricacies of network protocols and advancing your career in the field of networking.

www.ingramcontent.com/pod-product-compliance
Lightning Source LLC
Chambersburg PA
CBHW071235050326
40690CB00011B/2130